INSTANT IMPACT

INSTANT IMPACT

over 200 ideas for the
weekend decorator

Caroline Atkins

Project concepts by Amanda Morrison

WARD LOCK

A WARD LOCK BOOK

First published in the UK 1999 by
Ward Lock
Wellington House
125 Strand
London WC2R 0BB
www.cassell.co.uk

A Cassell Imprint

DESIGNED AND EDITED BY GLS EDITORIAL & DESIGN
Art director Ruth Shane
Editorial director Jane Laing
Contributing editors Claire Calman, Helen Ridge

Distributed in the United States by
Sterling Publishing Co., Inc.
387 Park Avenue South
New York NY 10016-8810

British Library Cataloguing-in-Publication Data
A catalogue record for this book is available from the British Library

ISBN 0-7063-7786-9

Colour separation by Tenon & Polert Colour Scanning Ltd.
Printed in Hong Kong

CONTENTS

Introduction
7

Walls & Floors
9

Space & Storage
43

Decoration
& Display
67

Curtains
& Blinds
91

Soft
Furnishings
117

Decorator's Essentials
129

Stockists & Suppliers
138

Index
140

INTRODUCTION

A change has come over decorating in the last few years. It's partly because more and more of us are 'doing it ourselves', so we want simpler techniques, more shortcuts and faster results. But it's also because new looks are coming around so fast that our old ones seem to be out of fashion almost before we've got used to them. Either way, the prevailing mood is for decorating ideas that make an instant impression – that give the room a completely new image without calling in a whole team of builders, plasterers and interior designers.

And that's what *Instant Impact* is all about – to let you be your own interior designer. A compilation of inspiring ideas and practical projects, this book shows you how to transform walls, floors, windows and furnishings – all in less than a weekend.

Instant Impact means keeping it easy, so you don't need any specialist skills. Some of the projects call for basic sewing or do-it-yourself ability, but the instructions are simple and easy to follow. The tools and materials needed for each one are clearly listed, and practical tips and additional design ideas are also given.

If you want to test the water before launching into a complete bathroom or kitchen makeover, then begin by trying out one of the smaller projects. It doesn't take more than a new treatment for a window or a few imaginative accessories to rejuvenate a tired room or furnishing scheme, and we've included quick ideas using paint, fabric and decorative trims as well as larger-scale revamps that conjure up an entirely different look. You could even create a new kitchen – without buying new units.

Decorating has never been more fun, so just pick your project and enjoy yourself...

WALLS & FLOORS

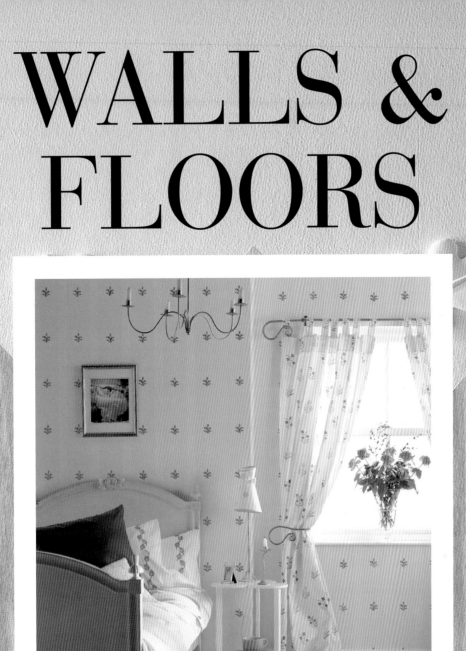

Bored with tired decorating schemes and lifeless rooms? Transform them with clever effects and simple paint techniques. No experience needed!

First impressions

Customize your walls to create this **delightfully romantic** bedroom, using a **rubber stamp** with a charming **leaf motif** combined with soft **neutrals** and **pretty** fabrics.

mix & match

Many people are rather wary of mixing different patterns in the same room, but it can be highly effective. The trick is to keep within the same broad style and colour range, so that the patterns are complementary, not conflicting. Here, the spirals on the lampshade and the sprigs on the curtains seem exactly right with the stencilled leaves on the walls.

For a room scheme that really is yours and yours alone, hand-print your walls with a simple, stylized motif. For this bedroom, a pre-cut rubber stamp was used (available from craft and decorating stores), but you may prefer to make one to your own design. You can use a stencil instead (for designs, see page 134), but a stamp gives a more hand-finished result, with more textural interest than the flat impression produced by a stencil.

To provide a good background for a hand-decorated finish, avoid anything too fussy and keep ornaments to a minimum. This classic, striped wallpaper in neutral tones provided a framework and guide for applying the stamp. On a plain wall, the effect might have been too 'dotty', but the stripes help to create a cohesive, well-balanced design.

In a light and summery bedroom, warm-toned neutral colours such as ivory and palest coffee are used as a foil for artistic touches of strong colour on the hand-stamped walls, sprigged curtains and decorated lampshade.

make your mark

Once you have tried your hand at stamping, you may want to use this simple yet effective technique in other ways or other rooms. Try it on plain calico for customized curtains or cushion covers, or on a simple parchment lampshade. Take care not to get carried away: if you stamp too many surfaces in one room, you may end up feeling you've been gift-wrapped!

stay in neutral

This bedroom illustrates just how well neutral tones complement the use of decorative pattern. Keep the floor covering and linens fairly simple, and let the other surfaces work as a low-profile backdrop so that they don't compete with the stamped walls.

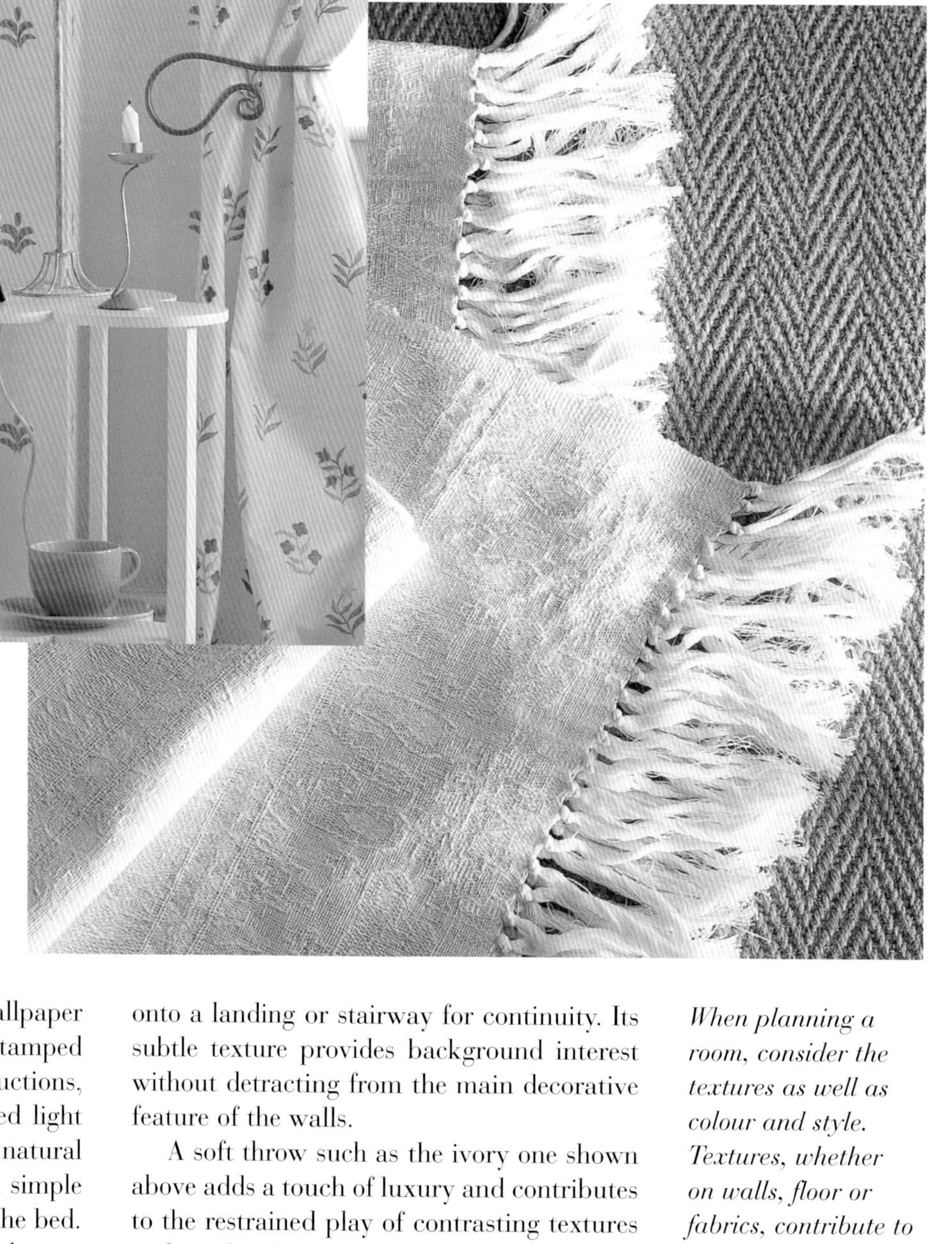

For this romantic, airy bedroom, the first step was to paper the walls in a striped wallpaper, but you can paint or colourwash stripes yourself as a background if you prefer (see pages 18–19). Next, paint the skirting board and window frame; we used cream paint to give the room a soft and pretty background colour for a bright, summery look. The wallpaper was then customized with hand-stamped motifs (see the step-by-step instructions, right) and gilt touches, and we added light floral-sprigged curtains. A durable natural matting was used for the floor and a simple pale rug added for extra comfort by the bed.

This herringbone matting provides an extremely hard-wearing, practical surface, ideal if you want to extend the flooring out onto a landing or stairway for continuity. Its subtle texture provides background interest without detracting from the main decorative feature of the walls.

A soft throw such as the ivory one shown above adds a touch of luxury and contributes to the restrained play of contrasting textures without battling against the patterns on the walls and curtains; it can be draped over the bed or an easy chair or screen.

When planning a room, consider the textures as well as colour and style. Textures, whether on walls, floor or fabrics, contribute to the overall pattern of the effect.

How to rubber stamp your walls

If you are not experienced at using a rubber stamp, first try out the stamp on a sheet of paper. The size of your square measuring card depends on the width of the stripes of the background paper. If applying stamps on a plain background, simply decide on the spacing you prefer, and make your measuring card accordingly.

You will need

thin card

emulsion paint

small paint roller

leaf-shaped rubber
   wall stamp

fine paintbrush

gold paint

1 First mark the position of each stamp. Cut out a piece of card to the required size — ours was 18cm (7¼in) square — and hold it diagonally against the wall as shown so that it forms a diamond shape. Place the bottom corner on the skirting board, in the centre of a wide stripe. Mark the wall with a pencil at the top point of the diamond. Move the diamond up so that its bottom corner is on the pencil mark and mark the top again. Continue until you have marked out all the stripes.

2 Pour the emulsion for the stamp colour into a paint tray. Gather paint on the roller and apply to the stamp. Make a few test prints on paper first so that you become confident about making an even impression with the stamp; this will also help you gauge the right amount of paint to use. Using the pencil marks as central points, stamp your pattern onto the wall, reapplying the paint on the leaf stamp each time.

3 Leave the stamped leaf impressions to dry. You may want to touch up any very uneven stamps, but resist the temptation to try to make every single impression perfect — the occasional flaw is all part of the hand-printed charm. With a fine brush, add a few lines of gold paint (available from art shops) to each leaf motif.

Spring greens

Be sure not to overlook the **smallest** room in the house. Here, a traditional, **patterned** wallpaper is brought right **up to date** with a cool, green colourwash and **stylish** detailing.

Bringing a fresh touch of spring into the home, this bathroom has been given a decorating scheme that suits its small proportions perfectly. The approach is quite restrained and formal, in contrast to that used for the chequerboard bathroom shown on pages 36–7.

The starting point and dominant pattern stem from the wallpaper with its stylized tree motif that would look equally at home in a country cottage or a city apartment. You can create a similar effect by making your own stamp or stencil on a cream painted base (see page 13 for how to print a pattern using a rubber stamp, and page 20 for instructions on using a stencil).

The random band of tiles uses complementary colours, forming a distinctive border between the patterned paper below and the green wall above. The floor has been kept plain, using pale, sealed plywood as a foil for the colour and pattern on the walls. The red check wastebin and the ribbon tying the coordinating blind (see page 111 for how to make the blind) add a touch of contrasting colour.

a light touch

When deciding on a paint colour for walls, consider the room's aspect, which affects the amount and quality of light. Check the natural light at different times of the day and note whether it is warm or cool light. For example, in a room that receives warm-toned evening sun, you can enhance the light with paintwork in peach and terracotta shades.

Strong colours and bright accessories are used with flair to create a fresh, pretty room that is decorative without being overwhelming.

How to apply colourwash

You will need

green matt emulsion
    paint
water
bucket
wide paintbrush or
    colourwash brush

Preparation

Paper the lower part of the walls to align with the top of the basin. Paint the upper half of the walls in cream as a base for the wash and leave to dry. Fix the tiles above the paper, starting at the basin.

1 To make up the green colourwash, mix equal amounts of your chosen matt emulsion paint with water in a clean bucket. Make sure that the two are well mixed before applying.

2 Gently brush the paint backwards and forwards, changing the angle of your stroke constantly. Keep stirring the colourwash in the bucket or it will tend to separate. Overlap your brush strokes again and again to achieve good coverage.

15

A grand entrance

This hallway strikes just the right balance between **formal** and **fun** with bold **colourwash stripes**, stairs stained a complementary shade of blue and **witty touches** of style.

When it comes to decorating, the entrance hall or lobby is often left to last and then given no more than a cursory lick of paint. But this is the first room to greet you when you arrive home – and the first one your visitors see – so it is well worth planning it as a welcoming space. This striking decorating treatment uses the drama of broad, contrasting stripes – ideal where you want to increase the sense of vertical space. It suggests the carefree feel of a celebratory marquee, with a note of Regency formality.

In this hallway, eclectic accessories and furnishings are combined to continue the mix of formal and casual: a traditional-style, crystal-drop chandelier hangs against the backdrop of a simple Roman blind and softly gathered gingham pelmet. A contemporary wirework shelf is juxtaposed with traditional botanical prints. Two miniature imitation box plants echo the ornamental, formal theme; and a neat set of miniature office drawers has been fixed to the wall to provide practical storage for going-out accessories.

Strong or large-scale patterns are best used in light, generously proportioned spaces, otherwise they may seem overwhelming.

beneath your feet

For the floor in a hall, lobby or landing, wood laminate flooring is highly practical: it is durable and easy to clean as well as attractive. Many types, such as the knotted pine effect shown here, are readily available in easy-to-lay panels.

How to paint colourwash stripes

You will need
emulsion paint
spirit level
masking tape
medium paintbrush or
   colourwash brush

1 First paint the wall in your chosen base colour, the paler shade of the stripes. Using a spirit level to get a true vertical, mark the position of the stripes. Use masking tape at the outside edges of the lines to be colourwashed. Mix equal proportions of paint and water and apply with a brush in random strokes. Work quickly from top to bottom, completing each stripe before moving on to the next.

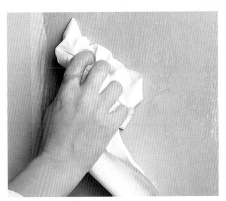

2 Keep stirring the colourwash to ensure an even mixture of paint and water. Use a soft cloth to wipe off any excess paint. Once it is dry, peel off the masking tape and touch up any uneven lines.

Falling leaves

You don't have to spend a fortune to **redecorate**. The walls and floor of this study-bedroom were quickly **revamped** using no more than a couple of pots of paint, a **simple stencil** and a little **imagination**...

hands-on project

For a children's playroom or nursery, try this playful idea – instead of a stencil, use a child's handprint, or a mixture of child and adult prints. This works well in a clearly defined area such as a border above the skirting or in an alcove where the toys are kept.

Vast stretches of plain wall can look bleak in a bedroom, but even the most boring wall can be rejuvenated with a stencil. We used a very simple leaf motif, stencilled in a pastel blue, to create a pretty yet restrained effect that doesn't look out of place with this alcove office.

Few people can spare enough space for a separate study, but working on a corner of the kitchen table is rarely satisfactory. If you have to accommodate functional desk space into a bedroom, living room or hallway, coordinate it as part of the overall scheme so it doesn't appear as an afterthought. Here, the storage accessories have been cleverly chosen to complement the feel of the bedroom (see pages 58–9).

Stencils are available in an enormous range of designs and styles, such as classical, Scandinavian and geometric, or you can make your own, as shown on the following page (see page 134 for template). An alternative to stencilling is to use a rubber stamp (see pages 10–13).

out of sight

If you prefer to hide away your workspace when you're not using it, add a lightweight curtain or simple blind across the whole working area, which won't intrude on the available space. Choose a fabric that complements the paintwork colours or match the existing curtains or blinds at the window to ensure the harmony of the scheme.

Leaf-stencilled walls and a classic chequerboard painted floor create a room that is both practical and attractive, with a serene colour scheme to soothe you at the end of a long day.

How to stencil a wall

Decide on the distance of your pattern repeat —
how far apart you want to place the stencils.
This depends on the overall proportions of the
room, the size of the stencil motif and your
chosen paint colour. For a dense pattern, keep
the repeat quite small; for an airier look, space
the designs further apart.

1 Trace the leaf design (see page 134) onto a
piece of stencil card, then cut out the shape
using a sharp craft knife (work on a mat or board
to protect surfaces). Cut a cardboard square with
sides the same size as your desired pattern repeat
— our repeat is 25cm (10in) so the cardboard
square we made was 25 x 25cm (10 x 10in).

2 Use a plumb line (see page 37) to
determine a true vertical and keep the
pattern straight. Fix the plumb line to the wall
and place the card on top as shown. Mark each
of the four corners. Move the square up so the
bottom corner is now at the mark originally
made for the top. Continue until you have
marked from floor to ceiling. Then work across
the wall, aligning corners with previous marks to
create an evenly spaced grid.

tonal contrasts

Bear in mind that the stronger the contrast
between the colour of the stencil and that of the
background, the more eyecatching and
emphatic the finished pattern will be. In general, for a large area, a minor contrast tends to
work very well, such as a pastel shade on a
white or stone-coloured background. In a
restricted space, such as cupboard doors or a
small cloakroom, a strong contrast may be very
striking — try burgundy or bottle green on
cream or ivory, or black on a primary colour.

3 To make the pastel shade for the leaf motif, mix two shades of
emulsion paint in a small bucket, using a ratio of 30 percent mid-blue
to 70 percent white. Align the leaf's stalk with each of the marks on the
wall. Secure the stencil with masking tape. Apply paint with a stencil brush,
and repeat the process until you have covered the entire area.

You will need

stencil card
craft knife
plumb line
string
emulsion paint
masking tape
stencil brush

Tiling a room with ceramic or even vinyl tiles can be expensive; creating the same effect with paint is a fraction of the cost.

Painting a chequerboard floor

Make sure you prepare your floor before painting. If painting floorboards or plywood flooring, you will need to use an undercoat or primer. Hardwearing floor paints are best for concrete or screeded floors but they are available in only a limited range of colours.

✳ To paint the floor in a chequerboard design, first decide on the size of the squares, which should be in proportion to the overall dimensions of the room. Protect any area you do not want to paint with masking tape. Apply two or three coats of the paler shade of emulsion and leave to dry.

✳ Starting in the centre of a wall, work outwards, marking out the floor into squares with chalk. Use a set square to ensure corners are accurate.

✳ Fix masking tape along the guidelines to create perfectly straight edges. Using the other colour, paint in alternate squares. Once the floor is completely dry, apply several coats of quick-drying acrylic varnish.

plotting a path

When painting a floor pattern, always start at the farthest point from the door and work towards the door so that you don't paint yourself into a corner. If the checks are large enough, you can use the dry ones as stepping stones should you need to cross the room.

Bathing in style

Lie back in the lap of luxury in this **opulent** bathroom with classical touches, mixing painted panelling, **gold calligraphy** and flowing curtains for a **sumptuous**, theatrical appeal.

With its curlicued iron shelving, Renaissance-style pictures and baroque, gilded mirror, this bathroom has a dramatic, classical feel. Colours are restrained, with cool blues and soft creams and yellows working in harmony. Star-spangled curtains, dyed using a simple batik technique, spill generously onto the floor (see pages 96–7 for instructions on how to make them).

The pale, sealed wood flooring and skirting board provide a neutral and unobtrusive background for any kind of bathmat or rug. Other accessories are kept deliberately simple, with glass bottles spaced evenly along the display shelf.

written in gold

Calligraphy or decorative lettering gives an extra dimension to a design because it can add a message as well as ornamental value. Choose words that reflect the purpose of the room, as shown here, or take a line from a favourite poem. Magazines and newspapers are a good source of stylish lettering or use the alphabets printed at the back of this book. Enlarge the letters on a photocopier to the size you want.

1 To make the stencil, carefully cut out the letters from the paper using a craft knife or scalpel for a neat finish. First chalk a guideline and the position of the letters on the wall to determine the spacing.

2 Use masking tape to attach the stencil to the wall and protect any areas that might be sprayed accidentally.

3 Carefully spray over the lettering using gold spray paint, leave to dry for a few minutes, then peel off the stencil.

How to create a classical bathroom

✳ First mark out the wall horizontally into three sections. Tile the bottom section, setting the tiles diagonally to create a diamond pattern.

✳ Now panel the middle section. You could use MDF (particleboard) or planed timber for the surround combined with tongue-and-groove boards (ask for fitting instructions where you buy the boards) fixed to the wall with building contact adhesive.

✳ Paint the panelling. Cream washable emulsion was used for the tongue-and-groove, ice blue for the surround and mid-blue for the bath panel.

✳ Attach the shelf with brackets set at intervals along the top edge of the MDF (particleboard) panel and screw the pre-painted shelf in place. Finish by applying the gold lettering (see left).

This sumptuous bathroom was created with canopy-curtaining, an ornate mirror and painted panelling. Gold touches from the lettering, mirror and picture frames add to the sense of luxury.

Flight of fancy

A **quick**, practical solution doesn't have to be short on style. Low on cost but high on impact, this **pattern** from a **simple stencil** on painted woodwork turns an ordinary flight of steps into a **talking point**.

When it comes to floorcoverings, stairs often present quite a challenge. Carpeting needs to be very tough if it is to look good with wear, but it can be expensive and tends to harbour dust or become marked. Bare wooden steps are easy to look after but may feel unwelcoming. This decorative approach is both stylish and practical – and it's easy to change when you want a new look.

For these stairs, a coin was used as the template to stencil a row of spots on each step. A strongly contrasting shade helps to delineate the treads clearly, a valuable safety plus in homes with poorly lit stairs. A simple shape is usually most effective; try diamonds, squares or a stylized leaf motif. To link an adjoining hallway or landing, you can repeat the stencil around the floor area or above the skirting as a border. If you will need to use the stairs while the paint is drying, work on alternate steps first, then paint the rest once these are dry.

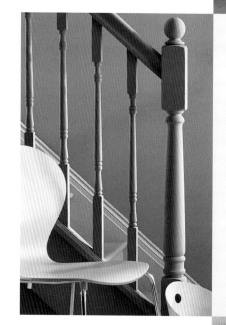

stylish steps

Here are some other ideas to try when decorating steps:
• Paint the treads in one colour and the risers in a different shade for a dramatic, jazzy effect.
• On plain, pale wooden stairs, apply a stencil using varnish in a deeper shade rather than paint.
• If the stairs have a narrow runner down the centre, make a painted border on either side freehand or using a stencil.
• For a tougher finish, use exterior paint or floor paint.

This hand-stencilled flight of stairs has a contemporary appeal, with a clean, uncluttered look in crisp blue and white. Painting the skirting a contrasting colour adds definition and gives emphasis to the spots.

Stencilling a stairway

To determine the best size of stencil for your stairs, cut out shapes from paper in different sizes to check the effect. When cutting the card for the stencil, you may find it easier to use an actual coin as a guide for the knife rather than a tracing of it.

You will need

card

coin or pastry cutter   paint
    as a template   stencil brush
craft knife or scalpel   clear varnish

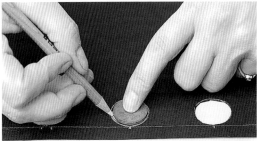

1 Cut a piece of card the same width as the stair tread. Using a coin or small pastry cutter as a template, mark out a line of evenly spaced circles.

2 Using a sharp craft knife, carefully cut out each circle. When you've cut out all the circles, tape the card to the step and apply paint with a small stencil brush. Use two or three thin layers of paint rather than one thick layer. Carefully remove the card, and once the paint has dried, give the stairs several coats of clear varnish for a really tough finish.

Seaside chic

Roughly plastered walls, **colourwashed** panelling and **shell-stencilled tiles** give this bathroom a **fresh,** seaside look with a **contemporary** twist. Practical duckboards prevent slips and protect the wooden floor – and create a strong **maritime** feel.

If you are stuck with uneven walls, you can combine two practical and stylish solutions, using tongue-and-groove panelling to dado height, with rough, painted plaster above. The effect is unpretentious – distinctive yet unfussy. This understated backdrop acts as a foil for the more dramatic wooden pelmet; running the length of the room, this provides a bold, decorative frame as well as concealing the shower curtain rail. Further, textural detailing comes from the bas-relief tiles, which have been stencilled with a spiral to suggest the form of a seashell or ammonite. Use accessories imaginatively to complement your central theme.

Here, a palette of mixed blues helps you steer clear of a contrived, over-coordinated look. Traditional seating in the form of a Lloyd Loom armchair and Van Gogh-style rush seat establish a relaxed feel. Storage is kept very simple: a plain shelf with wooden knobs provides useful space for accessories.

Sand and sea colours, rough textures and subtle use of detail combine to give this bathroom a coastal flavour.

curtained off

When attaching the pelmet to the ceiling, align it with the outer edge of the bath panel. After painting it, fix the shower curtain rail, either to the pelmet itself or suspended from the ceiling, concealing it behind the pelmet, and hang the shower curtain.

keeping dry

Shower curtains are easy to make but you will need to line your fabric with plastic backing if you use one that is not waterproof. Alternatively, set up a double rail to take an inner, waterproof curtain and an outer, decorative one for which you can use any material you like.

Colourwash panelling

You will need

tongue-and-groove
    panelling
length of 12 x 2.5cm
    (5 x 1in) wooden shelf
sandpaper
blue cold water dye or
    coloured wood stain
paintbrush
wood sealant or clear
    polyurethane varnish

※ Attach the tongue-and-groove panelling according to the supplier's instructions. Pin a batten to the top edge of the tongue-and-groove and screw the shelf into it.

※ Rub down the tongue-and-groove with sandpaper and clean well. Allow to dry.

※ Dissolve the contents of one pot of blue cold water dye in water, according to the instructions on the packet, and stir well. (Use a type suitable for staining wood; alternatively, use a coloured wood stain.)

※ Apply the solution to the boards with a brush or experiment with different effects using a sponge or cloth. Allow to dry. Finish with a couple of coats of wood sealant or clear polyurethane varnish.

Colourwashing the timber panelling brings out the subtle grain of the wood, contrasting with the varied textures of the rush seat, plaster wall and soft towels.

How to relief-stencil tiles

You will need

15 x 15cm (6 x 6in) ceramic tiles
firm card or acetate
scalpel or craft knife
textured paste

emulsion paint
fine paintbrush
plus
tile adhesive
tile grout

3 Carefully remove the stencil from the tile and leave it to dry in a warm place — any excess paste can be scraped off the stencil while it is still wet and re-used. Wipe down the stencil with a damp cloth before repeating the process on the rest of the tiles. When the paste is dry — this will take around four hours — place the stencil over the tile again and paint the raised area with the pale blue emulsion.

Apply the stencilled tiles at random intervals onto the bath panel with tile adhesive and grout, available from do-it-yourself and hardware stores.

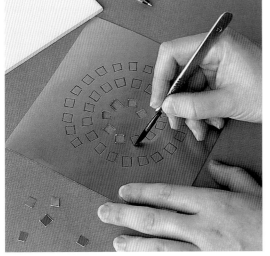

1 To make a template, cut a piece of firm card or acetate to the same dimensions as the tile. Trace the outline of your stencil design in the centre of the card. Cut out the shape using a sharp scalpel and hold the prepared stencil in position over the tile.

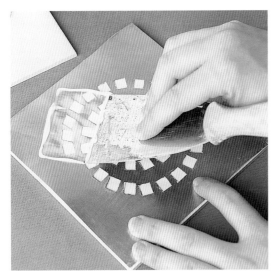

2 Apply textured paste, available from craft and decorating stores, over the surface of the stencil using a palette knife. Be careful not to press the paste down — it should be smoothed on as if you were icing a cake.

Cutting edge

Paint doesn't have a monopoly when it comes to **special effects**. Wallpaper can be far more **versatile** than you imagined. The following three schemes show just how **creative** you can be, with **smart zigzags**, delicate **découpage** and rustic **patchwork** designs.

To keep things simple, choose a plain or striped wallpaper because you won't need to line up the pattern repeat. Of course, there is nothing to stop you using a wallpaper with a more elaborate pattern repeat, but you will need to match each piece before cutting the shaped top. Rather than papering to the full height of the room, you will achieve a more distinctive effect if you allow some space at the top. In this zigzag scheme, a row of plaster-moulded leaves were used, which were painted with emulsion to match the wall (see pages 80–7 for more ideas on decorative mouldings). Alternatively, you can hang the wallpaper from a dado or picture rail.

using leftovers

For a more formal treatment, you can create a panelled effect on a wall with rectangles of wallpaper edged by moulding or beading. Paint the surrounding wall in a complementary shade or the same colour as the background of the wallpaper. If you have only a roll of paper to play with, make a frieze about 8–20cm (3–8in) deep to paste around the room.

For this sitting-room, an ordinary striped wallpaper has been given a contemporary twist by cutting the edge into a zigzag shape. This edge also serves as border to half-frame the plaster leaf mouldings. A tall, upright, narrow shelving unit adds more vertical emphasis to echo the stripes.

Making a zigzag edge

You will need

wallpaper
thin cardboard for
   template

scissors or craft knife
chalk
spirit level

1 To draw the zigzag pattern, first fold a piece of wallpaper in half lengthways and then fold the outside edges back to make three equally spaced folded lines. Draw a line across the wallpaper 15cm (6in) from the top edge. Then make the zigzag between this line and the top of the wallpaper.

2 Using scissors or a sharp knife, cut out along the pencil line. To create a template, transfer the zigzag shape to a piece of cardboard. Decide what height you would like the pattern, then cut lengths of wallpaper 5cm (2in) longer than this so that you can trim the lower edge neatly into the skirting.

3 Use the template to draw the shape onto each piece of wallpaper, then cut out the zigzag. Mark a horizontal line using chalk and a spirit level as a guide so that the upper zigzag points are aligned, and hang the wallpaper. Fix plaster shapes between the zigzags with double-sided self-adhesive pads, then paint them.

Delightful découpage

With some floral or highly patterned wall-papers, the effect can be over-fussy if you paper the entire room from floor to ceiling. One option is to use the wallpaper only as far as dado height, and paint the rest of the wall in a shade that picks out a colour from the paper. Adding a dado rail provides a neat division between the patterned and plain parts of the wall.

In this room, an innovative touch is the découpage frieze, using parts of the pattern cut out from the wallpaper. For best effect, use a design with distinct shapes that you can cut out easily; large patterns are less fiddly to use than small, detailed ones. As well as flowers and leaves, patterns with geometric shapes such as diamonds can look highly effective. The frieze is very easy to make, but make sure you cut out plenty of pieces before you start pasting them onto the wall – nothing is more frustrating than running out when you're only halfway through the job.

To liven up this bare expanse of bedroom wall above the dado rail, a pretty découpage frieze has been pasted on at picture rail height.

You will need

patterned wallpaper
scissors or craft knife
chalk
spirit level
wallpaper paste
paper towels

screen star

A very pretty idea for a bedroom, per-haps to conceal a study area or sewing table, is a découpage screen. An old screen that is rather the worse for wear can be given a new lease of life with découpage. Create a patchwork effect with geometric shapes of wallpaper in different patterns or textures but sticking to a limited colour palette.

1 Cut out a selection of shapes or motifs, such as whole flowers and leaves, from the wallpaper. Work out roughly how many you will need, but make sure you have some spare.

2 Decide on the position of the border and mark up the wall to give yourself a straight guideline, using chalk and a spirit level. Lay out the pieces on a flat surface to design the arrangement.

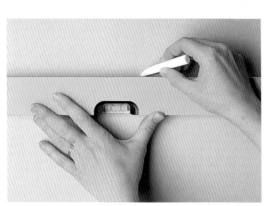

3 Using the chalk line as a guide, stick the shapes to the wall with wallpaper paste. Press in place with a piece of folded paper towel to mop up the excess paste. When the effect is complete, wipe away the chalk line with a damp cloth.

Check it out

This retro patchwork effect recreates the passion for pattern of the 1970s. It looks great in small areas such as a hallway or cloakroom. for part of a larger room. such as an alcove or chimneybreast, or as a dado at the bottom of the wall, up to waist height.

The ideal solution for using up odd, left-over rolls of wallpaper. this technique can also be used to make a border of alternating checks, perhaps around the walls near the ceiling as a frieze or to frame a doorway. Think twice before applying it to a large area because it can be overwhelming.

Consider decorating a child's or teenager's bedroom with patchwork checks: encourage them to help make the squares. For best results. stick to two different colourways of the same design and choose simple. small-scale patterns. Dense areas of colour tend to look more effective than delicately traced designs. You can also experiment with the size of the patchwork squares.

Customize wallpaper with this playful chequerboard effect created with two different colours of wallpaper in the same design.

How to patchwork a wall

You will need

wallpaper in two
   designs
scissors or craft knife
plumb line
wallpaper paste

1 Decide on the size of the squares; ours were 25 x 25cm (10 x 10in). Draw a guide every 25cm (10in) across the width of standard wallpaper and cut.

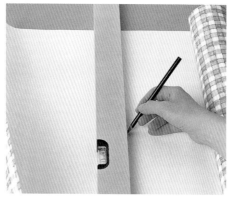

2 Fold the cut pieces of paper in half and cut out carefully to make two squares. Starting at one corner of the wall, use a plumb line to draw a vertical guideline on the wall 25cm (10in) from the corner. Fix the squares in alternating colours to the wall with wallpaper paste, aligning the edges carefully.

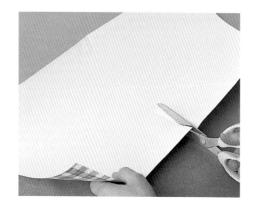

patch it up

You can also use this patchwork technique for items of furniture such as a child's toy-box; as the area to cover is small, the squares can be stuck on with paper glue instead of wallpaper paste. If the patch-work is applied as mock tiles to the side panel of a bath, the paper should be protected with two or three coats of clear varnish or sticky-backed plastic film.

A square deal

Definitely not for the hesitant, this **bold, painted** check design sets a contemporary note. Try this unashamedly positive **style statement** in a bathroom or in the alcove of a small bedroom or study.

One of the great advantages of decorating the smallest room in the home is that you can let your imagination run away with you and have an enormous amount of fun at the same time. You can experiment with effects that you might not dare use on a larger scale or in a room where you entertain friends or sit and relax.

If you use a strong pattern over a large area, such as a wall or floor, don't be apologetic about it. Be definite, and you'll carry it off with panache. For accessories, you can echo either of the principal paint colours, or go for a strikingly contrasting shade. Here, the window blind echoes the check motif, but in a vibrant red (see page 111 for instructions on how to make it).

When working with a dominant pattern on the walls, keep the floor covering simple and fairly neutral, or the effect may be overwhelming. Try plain floorboards that have been sanded and sealed or stained or colourwashed in a subtle shade. If you do not have natural wood floors, thick plywood flooring, a plain linoleum or vinyl covering are all practical for a bathroom.

The 'game' theme created by the chequerboard paintwork is echoed by the playing-card suit hooks that have been used for hanging the simple check cloth blind.

trellis tip

An ordinary garden trellis panel, painted to tie in with the colour scheme, makes an original feature, and is useful for hanging small towels and bath accessories. The wooden grid of the trellis echoes the painted checks of the walls. Simply lean it against one wall, or fix it with screws, using small wood blocks or cotton reels behind it to hold it away from the wall.

How to paint the checks

You will need

cream matt emulsion paint

paint roller or broad
  paintbrush

plumb line

fine paintbrush

green matt emulsion paint

making a plumb line

A plumb line is a useful tool to have at hand when you need to create a perfect vertical line. You can make your own by attaching a fairly heavy object such as a ball of modelling clay or a bunch of keys to one end of a length of string so that it hangs straight down.

1 Paint the wall using the paler colour (here, cream matt emulsion) and leave to dry. Then, starting at the centre of the window, hang a plumb line from the ceiling to the floor. Make a pencil mark at the top and bottom of the string, then again down the wall at 20cm (8in) intervals. Move the plumb line along the wall 20cm (8in) and repeat the process until you have marked out the whole area you want to paint. Use a ruler to join up the marks.

2 Paint every alternate square with green matt emulsion: first, outline the square with a fine paintbrush. You may want to do this freehand, to emphasize the fact that the wall is hand painted. Alternatively, if you prefer perfectly straight lines, use masking tape for a crisp edge. Try to cover the pencil lines so that you don't have to erase them later on, or wait until the paint is completely dry before erasing them.

Perfect panelling

No period details? No problem. Even the dullest room can be **transformed** with **traditional panelling**, ranging from the formality of grand **townhouse** or **country-manor style** to simple shiplap or tongue-and-groove.

Add interest to a plain wall, or disguise an uneven or damaged one, with traditional panelling. Available in pre-cut panel sections, they come ready to be fixed to the wall. They may be covered with wood stain, colourwashed or painted; use matt, satin or eggshell paint in preference to gloss for best effect.

a question of style

Consider the overall style and period of your home before you decide whether to add panelling and which type to choose. Traditional, formal squared panelling is best suited to a fairly substantial home – though not necessarily a large room. Shiplap has a rustic feel, ideal for a country cottage or a simple retreat by the sea. Tongue-and-groove is the most versatile in terms of style, and can look as right in a rural or urban home, period or contemporary; its humble origins make it less appropriate for a very grand house.

Whether it's aged oak or painted tongue-and-groove pine, panelling always seems to add tremendous charm and style to a room. Few people may be fortunate enough to have these original features in their homes, but now anyone can enjoy them – without the expertise of a carpenter. It is easier to panel a wall than ever before, with a wide range of ready-made products including planed boards, prepared tongue-and-groove and entire panel sections, available from timber merchants (lumberyards) or decorating stores.

A decorative shelf trim can be painted to coordinate with panelling below or used on its own. Shelf trims are available pre-cut from good decorating stores, or you can cut one with a jigsaw to your own design in wood or MDF (particleboard). Remember to use a protective face mask if cutting MDF.

Add a touch of drama to a drawing-room, hallway or dining-room with confident use of intense colour, baroque-style furnishings and gilded detailing.

Perfect for a bathroom in a country or coastal setting, shiplap boarding has an unspoilt charm and is a refreshing alternative to tongue-and-groove.

As well as considering the style of panelling (see box, page 39), you need to think about its position in the room and colour tone. Some traditional panelling was originally used floor to ceiling, but nowadays this might seem like too much of a good thing. Panelling the lower walls only, as shown in the picture on the left, creates a strong impact but a much lighter effect that is more in tune with contemporary living. And while authentic dark panelling may make a room seem gloomy, painted wood still has a traditional feel but reflects the light much more successfully. In general, the larger the area of panelling, the lighter the colour should be.

Wall panelling is surprisingly versatile, and can look very different depending on whether it is painted, stained, colourwashed or simply sealed. Dividing the walls horizontally, with panelling up to dado height, allows you to use darker or more intense colours than when painting floor to ceiling. In the sitting-room shown on the left, the tongue-and-groove boards, skirting board and dado rail were painted with a deep burgundy paint. The overall effect is rich and slightly theatrical without being overpowering.

The addition of gold decorative mouldings gives the effect a lift, counterpointing the depth of colour of the paintwork (for more ideas on mouldings, see pages 77, 80–7). Ornate, wrought-iron furniture with baroque-style curlicues contributes to the stage-set atmosphere of the room. It was decided to cover the floor with a room-size patterned rug, to introduce a lighter colour in the lower part of the room, with the small-scale pattern serving to break up the intensity of the painted panelling.

ship-shape shiplap

Shiplap boards also look good if they are given a 'distressed' finish so that they seem weathered by age or, if they are outside, by the elements. One way to achieve this is to paint them, leave to dry, then lightly rub back the paint in places. Alternatively, paint a base coat of one colour, allow to dry, then add a top coat of a different colour. When semi-dry, rub back the paint in parts to allow streaks of the base colour to show through.

SPACE & STORAGE

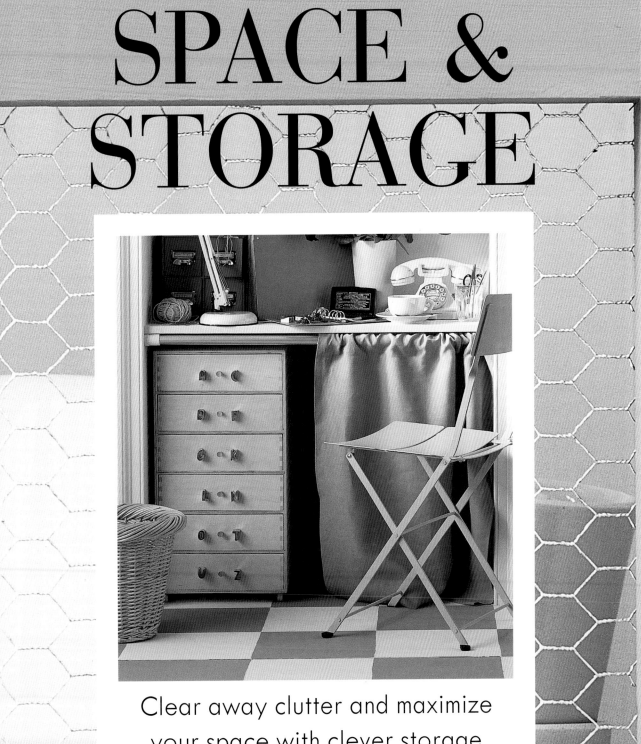

Clear away clutter and maximize your space with clever storage concepts and tricks to turn even the dullest cupboard into a stylish storage unit.

Sleek & modern

Finding enough **storage space** for all your **pots and pans** may seem virtually impossible. However, with a little **ingenuity** it can be done, **quickly** and **stylishly**, and without investing in a completely new kitchen.

The stunning modern makeover given to a tiny galley kitchen shows exactly how style and efficiency can be achieved on an extremely tight budget and in very little time.

This contemporary-style kitchen, with its ample storage, was achieved with a few cheap items from hardware and kitchen stores, and by adapting and recycling what already existed. Run-of-the-mill wall and floor cupboards have been customized by removing the door of one cupboard to show off good-looking storage jars and containers, and inexpensive streamlined doors have replaced the dull, original doors. Made of MDF (particleboard), the doors are plain and simple but given a strong, graphic edge by the sleek chrome handles.

Colour plays a major role in this kitchen. Vibrant acid yellows and greens introduce drama and bring the room firmly up to date, while the white worktop and woodwork provide light relief. The old cupboard doors have been salvaged to create made-to-measure shelving for the open cupboard. Once sawn, sanded and painted, the shelves were glued (they can also be pegged using plastic shelf supports) into the carcass.

An aluminium rail with metal hooks is stylish and eminently practical, keeping the stainless-steel utensils close to hand but off the worktop.

accessorize

Accessories can make or break a decorative scheme: frilled gingham curtains and wicker baskets, intrinsic features of the country kitchen, would be disastrous in a contemporary kitchen. Here, stainless-steel storage jars strike a modern pose alongside the retro metal toaster, while the long-legged metal chair introduces yet another streamlined and unfussy element to the room, helping to unify the scheme.

For a dramatic scheme with a contemporary twist, add a splash of colour to your kitchen by mixing bold acid brights with stainless-steel and plain white accessories.

Devious doors

If your kitchen is looking jaded, **new cupboard doors** are an easy way of giving it an **instant facelift**. Create your own **unique designs** with tiles, tin or fabric – or put your favourite china **behind bars** or a **mesh facade**.

Don't worry if you have never made a door before – step-by-step instructions tell you everything you need to know. Before starting any of the replacement door projects, make sure you check that the cupboard carcasses are in good condition. If the units themselves are damaged, the new doors will highlight the defects.

Each of the doors featured on the following pages is based on one of three designs – a simple frame, a plain piece of MDF (particleboard), and a Shaker-style combination of the two (see right). Be sure to prime the wood before painting – an acrylic primer will dry quickly. You will also need a staple gun, wood glue, masking tape and strong insulating or carpet tape, all available from hardware stores.

fixing hinges

To fit the doors to the carcass, you will need two easy-fit concealed hinges per door, available cheaply from most hardware stores. First, measure an equal distance from the top and bottom of the carcass, then mark exactly the same positions on the door itself. Using short screws at marked points, attach the hinges to the carcass. Hold the door in position, making sure it is at 90 degrees to the carcass frame, then drill and screw it into place.

To make the doors

Simple frame door

First, measure the height and width of the cabinet carcass or, if it is available, the old door. To make the vertical pieces of the frame, cut two lengths of timber 8 x 2.5cm (3 x 1in) – planed softwood is ideal – to the full height of the carcass. Repeat the process for the horizontal pieces. To calculate the right length, you need to take the width of the door and subtract the width of the two vertical pieces.

To join the vertical and horizontal pieces, drill a 13cm (5in) deep hole in the vertical pieces and countersink a 10cm (4in) screw to a depth of 2.5cm (1in), then glue and screw the frames together. For a stronger joint, drill a 12mm (½in) hole 2cm (¾in) from each end of the horizontal rails and glue in a short length of hardwood dowel.

Basic MDF panel

Measure the carcass or old door and ask your wood supplier to cut a rectangle of MDF (particleboard) to the same size.

Shaker-style door

Measure the carcass or old door. Cut a 'backing panel' to fit from a 9mm (⅜in) or 12mm (½in) thick MDF (particleboard) panel.

Using the simple frame door method (see above), make the frame from MDF off-cuts. Glue and pin these to the backing panel, and when the glue has dried, sandpaper the edges until there is no evidence of ridges between the panel and frame.

Two different styles and colours of cupboard doors, both very simple to make, have been combined to create a unique look for kitchen storage.

Heart to heart

This Shaker-style door is understated enough to be used on a whole kitchenful of cabinets.

Start with a Shaker-style door (see page 46). To attach the tongue-and-groove panelling, start at the centre of the door panel with a full-sized piece of panelling and work outwards, pinning each piece to the backing panel. Cut the two outside pieces to fit the spaces left.

To create the heart motif, place a template (see page 136) on the centre panel, outline the shape in pencil and cut out using a jigsaw. Sand the edges slightly to remove any splintered pieces. Paint the door and add a handle following the instructions given for the Mix & mesh door (see page 51).

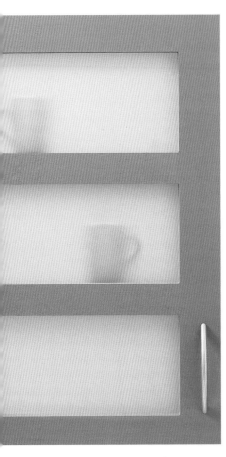

Cool & frosted

Clean-cut and sophisticated, this cupboard door creates a modern feel; if you want something a little bolder, consider tinted Perspex (Plexiglass). Pre-cut Perspex is available from signmakers and specialist hardware stores. It is worth asking for a scratch-resistant polycarbonate derivative.

Start with the basic MDF panel (see page 46). Plan the 'windows' in the door by trying out oblongs of paper in various sizes. Mark the chosen design in pencil and cut out the 'window' with a jigsaw. Sand the edges smooth.

Paint the frame. When dry, screw a sheet of frosted or opalescent Perspex (Plexiglass) onto the back of the door. Add a handle following the instructions for the Mix & mesh door (see page 51).

Net working

This cupboard front is ideal as a wall display cabinet. If you don't want all your china on show, you can have just one or two mesh fronts in a row of plain cupboards.

Make a simple frame door (see page 46) and paint. Measure the opening and cut chicken wire to size, leaving an extra couple of centimetres (an inch) all round for easy fixing. Fix the wire to the reverse side of the frame using a staple gun. (Different mesh sizes will give different effects.) Screw in a door knob and paint it to match the door.

Curtain call

You don't have to match the fabric for this door to your paint colour – try one of a similar tone. Gingham or check fabrics will create a traditional country look, or use plain muslin or calico.

Start with a simple frame door (see page 46) and paint it. Each door will need about a metre (one yard) of fabric. Cut the fabric to 1½ times the width of the cupboard door and make sure it is longer than the door to allow for a 1cm (½in) hem top and bottom.

Thread expandable curtain wires with eyelets through the hems and gather the fabric evenly along them. Fix two screws to the top and bottom of the inside frame and hook the wires over them. (Alternatively, you can staple the curtains to the frame, but the wires will make it easier to remove them for washing.) Add a wooden handle painted to match the cupboard.

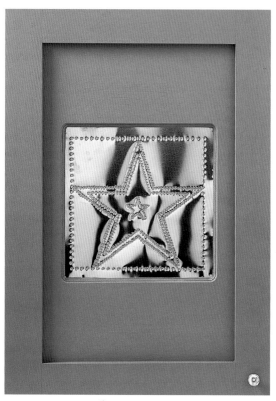

Starstruck

Personalize your kitchen with a punched motif, such as a star. All sorts of shapes and patterns can be used, from the very simple to the quite intricate.

Make a Shaker-style door (see page 46). Cut a piece of tin (available from metal merchants) to size with tin snips.

Draw a template of your design and attach it to the tin using tape. Punch holes into the sheet using a hammer and different-sized nails (put a lump of reusable adhesive or a cork mat behind the sheet to receive the nail).

Cut a hole in the door that is slightly smaller than the panel of tin. Paint the tin and then tack it to the back of the door. Place thick insulating tape over any sharp edges at the back and attach a handle to the corner of the door.

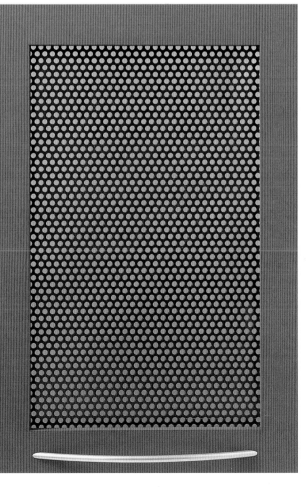

Behind bars

This cupboard front is well suited to both floor-standing and wall-mounted cabinets and looks particularly good alongside the hole-punched door (see left).

The design is based on the simple frame door (see page 46) but with dowels added to make the bars. These must be fitted before you assemble the frame.

Mark the dowel centres on the horizontal pieces of the frame about 5cm (2in) apart, and drill holes at these points. Glue the dowels in place and assemble the frame. Allow the glue to dry before painting and attaching the handle.

Mix & mesh

For a contemporary, minimalist look, fit a panel of sheet metal (available from metal merchants) to a painted frame and add a sleek chrome handle.

Make a simple frame door (see page 46) and paint it. With tin snips, cut a sheet of perforated steel to size and then screw or staple the steel to the back of the frame between the perforations. Fit the handle using a drill bit a little smaller than the screw shaft. Drill two holes through the panel from front to back. Put the handle in position and screw into place.

The final drill

The holes in this cupboard front can be as random or as regimented as you like – but try out different configurations on paper before you start drilling.

Make up a Shaker-style door (see page 46) and transfer a prepared template onto the surface. Drill holes using a 12mm (½in) drill bit, then paint the door. Finally, add a handle – a clover-leaf pull handle with a rust finish is shown here – see the instructions given for the Mix & mesh door on page 51.

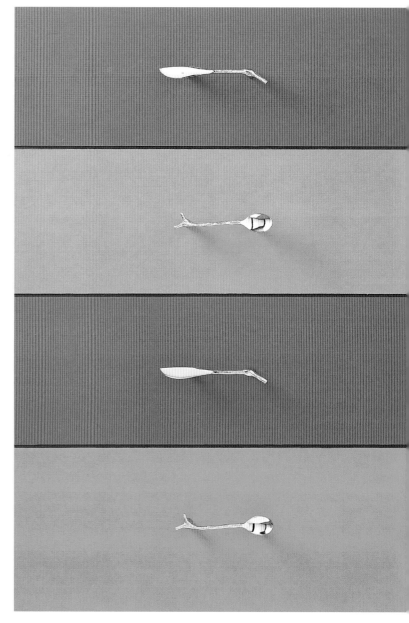

Trompe l'oeil

An easy trompe l'oeil paint effect in two colours can make plain kitchen cupboards look like drawer fronts.

Start by making a basic MDF (particleboard) panel (see page 46) and paint the whole surface with the paler colour. Block off areas with masking tape and paint in the remaining surface with the darker paint.

Define the drawers with a thin dark line between the two colours. Smudging the line slightly will give an illusion of gaps between the drawer. Attach the handles following the instructions given for the Mix & mesh door (see page 51).

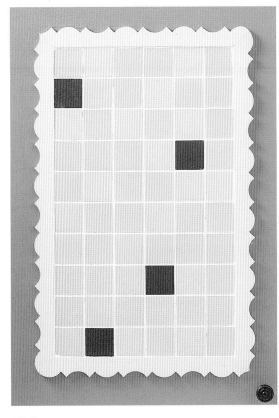

Tile it

Create a coordinated look by tiling your cupboard doors to match your walls.

On a basic MDF (particleboard) panel (see page 46), fix a rectangular chequerboard of tiles in the centre with tile cement and grout. Paint the surrounding area and leave to dry. Make the edge trims, or buy ready-cut MDF strips from do-it-yourself stores. Cut to size, paint, then glue around the tiles. Finally, attach a handle.

Playing chequers

Although extremely smart and chic, this chequerboard door couldn't be simpler to make. Painting the squares in more strongly contrasting shades than shown here will make the door even more of a feature in a modern kitchen.

Start with a Shaker-style door (see page 46) and paint it in the paler of your two colours. Mark the divisions in pencil, then, using masking tape for a clean line, paint alternate quarters in the darker colour. Finally, fit a handle, following the instructions given for the Mix & mesh door (see page 51).

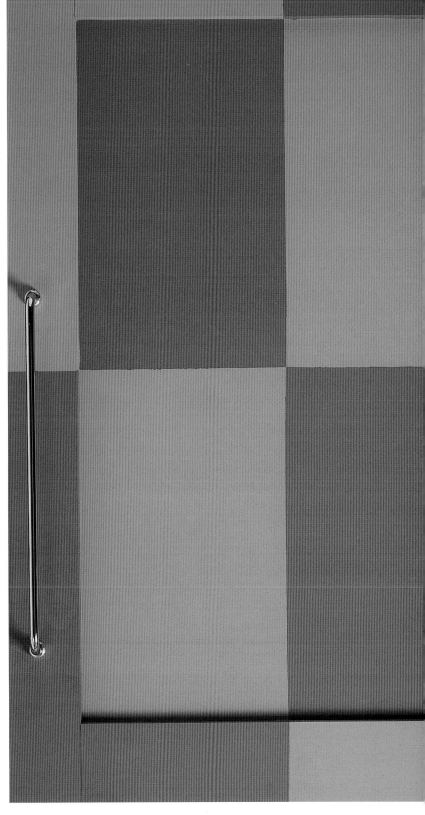

Shaker simplicity

This kitchen makeover creates an instant **Shaker-style** kitchen – **calm** and uncomplicated, **free of fuss** and frills. **Chicken-wire** door fronts reveal simply stacked china while checked **curtained cupboards** hide more functional items from view.

In this kitchen, the original, old doors to the floor cupboards have been removed and then replaced with curtaining threaded on to an aluminium rod (see opposite, top). Even with limited sewing skills, these curtains are very easy to make. Simply attach a metal rod with cup hooks at either end of the cupboard run – you may need one in the middle for extra support – and then make up a curtain 1½ times the length of the run. Eyelets fixed along the top edge at intervals allow the curtain to be threaded along the metal rod. Although the curtain will remain closed for most of the time, it is a good idea to paint the carcass of the floor cupboard the same colour as that of the wall cupboard, just for those occasions when all is revealed. Painting the kickboard red continues the colour theme.

The doors from the wall cupboards have also been removed, but not discarded. Instead, a square has been drawn in the centre of the door, leaving a 13cm (5in) border, and this shape cut out with a jigsaw and the edges sanded. Wooden beading was applied around the edge using wood glue, and then painted. A piece of chicken wire was cut slightly larger than the hole and fixed to the back of the door with a staple gun. New handles complete the look. The doors can then be fixed back on to the carcass with the original hinges.

This simple Shaker-style kitchen has curtained cupboards and chicken-wire door fronts. A peg rail, hand-painted tiles and galvanized accessories complete the all-American look.

storing herbs & spices

Even dried herbs and spices have a limited life-span but keeping them in air-tight containers helps to preserve them. Never store them by the stove: the heat will make them lose their pungency.

Red gingham curtains suspended from a metal rod make simple, practical cupboard fronts, and match the valance at the window.

If you're concerned that the open mesh will allow too much dust and dirt to enter the cupboard, fix a sheet of transparent Perspex (Plexiglass) to the inside of the door. Alternatively, if you like the effect created by the chicken wire but don't want to put the contents of your cupboard on display, stretch a piece of fabric across the back of the door behind the wire. Choose a white or very deep coloured fabric that will make a good backdrop and set off the grey of the wire.

All sorts of fronts can be added on to existing cupboards to give instant revamps: you can buy doors from kitchen and hardware stores or make them yourself without specialist skills. Glass-fronted doors are one option, allowing you to show off decorative china while keeping it free from dust and out of harm's way. Other cupboard fronts are featured on pages 46–53. More utilitarian objects can be kept hidden behind closed doors.

Making good use of leftovers, in this case a discarded floor cupboard door, prompted the creation of the Shaker-style peg rail. A 5cm (2in) wide piece of wood was cut to length from the door and at even intervals doorknobs were screwed in along the length. Painted and then attached to the wall with screws, it makes an out-of-the-way home for wooden salad servers, a chopping board and decorative lantern.

Office efficiency

More and more people **work from home** now than **ever before**. Even if you don't have a spare room to turn into a dedicated office, it is still possible to create a **comfortable** and **practical** working **environment** at home.

If your home office has been squeezed into an alcove or a corner of a room, then making the most of the space available to you is essential. Forward planning, organization and a little imagination – but not necessarily a great deal of money – will make it possible. The ideas given here are inexpensive, easy to achieve and guaranteed to make working at home more pleasant and efficient and therefore less stressful.

Choose your furniture and accessories with care: they should be pleasing to the eye as well as functional. A painted section of MDF (particleboard) bracketed to the wall with open shelves to either side takes up less space than a freestanding desk with pull-out drawers. A folding chair can be stored away on wall hooks (make a padded cushion seat with ties if you find the seat uncomfortable).

Wall space is often overlooked. Waste paper baskets can be hung from wall hooks, and magazines or posters stored in wall-mounted wire or wicker baskets or shiny metal boxes, to keep the floor free of clutter. They are also far more attractive than conventional office cardboard boxes. Scissors and home-made fabric pencil pots with tabbed holders (see main picture) can be hooked onto a rail to free up desk space.

keeping it simple

A piece of MDF (particleboard) can be cut to fit a specific space, then bracketed to the wall about 75cm (2½ft) from the floor to form an inexpensive and effective desktop. Add a second piece of wood, fixed about 1.6m (5½ft) from the floor, to form a shelf. Timber merchants (lumberyards) will cut the MDF to size for you, or you can buy pre-cut shelving.

take notice

This stylish noticeboard was made out of an old piece of chipboard covered in wadding and fabric, with the retaining ribbon held in place with upholstery tacks.

Cut out three or four layers of wadding and a piece of fabric slightly larger than the chipboard. Fix the wadding in place and then the fabric with a staple gun. Wrap ribbon across the board to form a trellis and fix on the reverse with staples or tacks. Trim the edges of the noticeboard with braid, glue a piece of felt on the back, screw in picture rings and fix to the wall.

Make a colourful noticeboard (see above) for safeguarding aide-memoires and photographs and storing stray paperclips. Flowers brighten up any office; if there is not enough room on the desk, put them in a wall vase.

It is probably true to say that you can never have enough shelves in a home office, so why not make use of the space above a door or alcove and build a couple of bookshelves? (Remember, you will probably need a small step-ladder to reach them, so these shelves are best reserved for books or files that you refer to less often.)

The utilitarian filing cabinet is an undisputed storage essential for most offices but its dull grey metal exterior can sit uncomfortably in a home office that forms part of another room. Spray painting it the same shade as the walls or a bright, eye-catching colour will transform its workaday image instantly. Replacing the handles will customize it still further; fixing heavy-duty casters to the bottom will give added flexibility, allowing you to hide the cabinet away under the desk when it's not needed and to pull it out for an extra work surface.

Created in a recessed space less than one metre (three feet) across, and with ingenious storage ideas, this home office is a practical and efficient working area. It is also attractive and unobtrusive enough for the corner of a bedroom.

Metal effects

Metal accessories and bright colours give the home office shown on this page a contemporary feel and, although created in the same space, it is in striking contrast to the more feminine home office shown on pages 56–7.

Unashamedly bold and uncompromising, it is also very easy to achieve and uses every inch of available space. Such a set-up would work well in a hallway – a couple of roller blinds fitted inside the top of the recess and at desk level would allow you to close off the office at the end of the day.

A variety of household equipment can be adapted for use in the home office. Wire or metal cooling racks hung on the wall and fitted with grid hooks make unusual storage for stationery items. Paint kettles or camping pots can be filled with pens, pencil and rulers and hung from hooks. Wire baskets can be attached to the underside of the desk for out-of-the-way filing, provided they do not get in the way of your knees.

Adjustable desk lamps are smart and versatile, provide good task lighting and take up precious little space. There are models that come supplied with clamp fittings. Fixed to an overhead shelf, they are even more space-saving and throw a wider beam of light.

Notoriously greedy for space, computer equipment is now a standard feature in most home offices. Fortunately, not all of the component parts are needed on the desk: the printer can sit on its own made-to-measure wall shelf close by, while the hard drive can be secreted away under the desk, but do take care not to kick it!

Shiny chrome accessories and state-of-the-art storage solutions create a smart, contemporary home office.

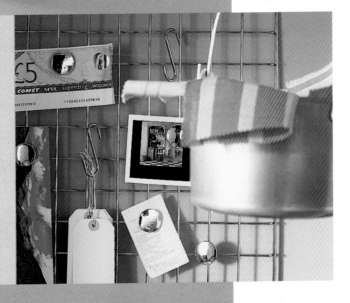

grid locked

A metal cooling rack from the kitchen doubles as an unusual and contemporary storage/display unit. Parcel labels are looped over 'S'-shaped hooks and chrome magnets keep notes and postcards close to hand but off the desk. A metal pan hanging from an overhead rail makes an original, out-of-the way holder for other odds and ends.

An extending pole, made of either wood or metal and sandwiched between two vertical supports, can be used as a curtain rail (see pages 56–7) or as a runner for attaching chrome hooks, to create flexible and accessible storage (see pages 58–9).

Freeing the desk area from extraneous items of stationery and other odds and ends is essential for unimpeded work. Paperwork can be filed away on hooks screwed into the wall; in this office, alphabet cake cutters above daisy-shaped hooks indicate 'In' and 'Out'. A metal rail with chrome hooks, complementing the metallic shelf and boxes above, provides additional storage away from the desk (see above).

Metal accessories bring this home office right up to date. Alphabet-shaped cake cutters glued onto drawers serve to indicate the contents inside, making filing quick and easy.

Making a studded shelf

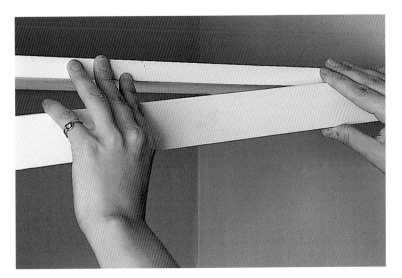

You will need
length of wood
panel pins
upholstery tacks
emulsion paint
paintbrush

1 Cut a strip of wood, approximately 9cm (3½in) deep, to the same length as the shelf.

2 Line up the top of the strip of wood with the top of the shelf. Tack the strip in place with three or four panel pins. Decorate the shelf trim by driving in upholstery tacks.

3 When satisfied that you have the right number of tacks, apply a couple of coats of emulsion paint to the trim and tacks.

A plain wooden shelf is given an interesting boxy look with the addition of a painted wooden trim decorated with upholstery pins.

Flexible storage

Without enough **storage space**, our lives would be cluttered and disordered. Boxes comes in all **shapes, sizes** and **materials** – perfect for **concealing** and **protecting** those possessions not meant to be on public display.

The pictures shown here illustrate how a set of small wooden boxes can be treated in different ways to make either practical storage drawers or an open display shelf.

Available from home furnishing stores, or easy to make yourself with 8mm (⅜in) plywood, panel pins and wood glue, the five drawers were first lightly sanded at the sides, top and bottom. This was to ensure that they would fit back into their holding box after being painted the same colour as the pale stripe on the wall (see right). The unit was then fixed under the hall window with screws and wall plugs. Brass name holders screwed onto each drawer identify their contents. A protruding dog lead reveals the use of one drawer; others can be used as a handy place to put house and car keys, driving licences, woolly hats and gloves, and so on.

As an alternative, the five drawers were completely removed from the wooden carcass. Less a unit for functional storage than for display, the shelf now houses tiny silver flowerpots but could be just as useful as a temporary resting place for newspapers, reminders, bills and circulars.

The drawers that were removed were put to good use. One was covered with blue gingham to make an attractive pencil pot. Painted and coated with exterior varnish, these box drawers make ideal plant pot holders (remember to drill drainage holes in the bottom), or use them for desk and kitchen tidies or for sewing equipment.

No one ever seems to have quite enough storage and, if you have very limited space

In this hallway, the drawers have been removed from a box storage unit to transform it into an open display shelf for pots and planters.

boxed in

Modular storage systems are stylish and efficient for every room in the home. Available from good furniture and do-it-yourself stores, they offer great flexibility, with a range of units in different shapes and sizes that can be combined in various ways according to your needs.

with which to work, you will need to use your imagination and lateral thinking. Sliding doors on cupboards take up less space than hinged doors, while a window seat fitted with drawers, doors or a lid can house bulky items such as blankets. Casters allow you to create mobile storage. They can be fixed to all sorts of storage units, from tea chests and trunks to home entertainment units and filing cabinets (see also page 57). For a contemporary look, fix a section of metal pipe at right angles to the bedroom wall and use it as a practical 'open' wardrobe for hanging clothes.

below stairs

Although an odd shape, the space under the stairs can be put to a surprising number of uses. It can accommodate built-in wine racks; made-to-measure drawers on runners for storing kitchen overspill such as food cans; a washing machine or freezer under the lowest part of the stairs and a broom and ironing board under the tallest; different-sized shelves for shoes and boots; or an open bookcase.

These discreet storage boxes make good use of an empty stretch of wall beneath the hall windowsill.

In the country

This bright blue **country** kitchen is refreshingly **unpretentious** and **workmanlike**. Equipment and utensils are close by, making meal preparation **easy** and **straightforward**.

The doors to both the wall and floor cupboards have been removed and the carcasses painted to reveal their contents. To give the cupboards a decorative edge, a shelf trim has been stuck on with wood glue and pins, and then painted.

Don't feel that all your appliances should be hidden away – kitchen storage is also about display. So many utensils look good as well as being functional, so make a feature of shiny pots and pans that you use fre-quently. Hang them from hooks on a metal pole run-ning above the sink or from hooks on a ceiling rail (make sure that the rail is high enough so that you don't keep hitting your head).

Where countertops are overflowing, make use of the wall space between the wall and floor cupboards. Wooden trellis (available cheaply from do-it-yourself stores and garden centres), which has been cut to size and painted, can be attached to the wall with screws and fitted with cup hooks. A standard white refrigera-tor may sit uncomfortably in a country-style kitchen, so why not hide it behind a piece of checked fabric? All you need do is measure the refrigerator door and cut and hem a piece of fabric to size. Then screw cup hooks into the work surface and hang the cover using a row of eyelets or buttonholes.

You don't need to spend huge amounts of money on interesting containers. Ask your greengrocer to put aside old fruit and vegetable crates for you. They make useful storage drawers for brushes, teatowels, even knives and forks. To make finding things easier, label the boxes with brass card holders or stencilled lettering.

By revamping conventional kitchen cupboards, using rustic storage crates and wooden trellis for 'display' storage, a country-style pantry has been created without breaking the bank.

DECORATION & DISPLAY

Indulge your imagination with delightful details and innovative ideas for transforming plain walls and features such as mirrors, tiles and shelves.

Tropical daydream

For a taste of the **tropics**, deck out a room with **starfish**, an **aquatic** mirror and **ocean-style** fabric. The bright turquoise walls add to the **Caribbean** atmosphere.

A light-filled bathroom is perfect for transforming into a tropical oasis. Bright Caribbean colours form the backdrop to this bathroom and unusual maritime decorations supply the finishing touches. For details of how to make the unusual rope-tied blind and the curtain for the bath panel, see pages 114–15.

The sea wave mirror makes a striking feature on the wall and is simple to make. Ask your local glass merchant to cut a piece of mirror to size and then glue it to the centre of a larger piece of ply-wood, at least 8cm (3in) all round. Whether you buy the wavy pelmet edging from a home furnishings store or make it yourself from MDF (particleboard) and a jigsaw, you will need to cut four lengths from the edging and mitre (cut at 45 degrees) the corners to fit the mirror, bearing in mind the pattern of the pelmet. Then, it needs to be painted: here, blue emulsion has been used to complement the walls. When dry, glue together the sections of the edging around the mirror, screw two hooks to the back and attach strong picture wire.

Dramatic shapes, vivid colours and beach-style accessories conspire to give this sunny bathroom a vibrant Caribbean feel.

How to make the starfish motifs

These plaster starfish motifs on the wall are quirky, decorative and very easy to make at home (see far right). A real starfish, often available from shell or seaside gift shops, is required to make the mould.

You will need

starfish
cake tin
aluminium foil
mould-making material
plaster of paris
emulsion paint
adhesive pads

1 Find a container large enough to hold the starfish, such as a cake tin, and line it with aluminium foil. Mix the mould-making material (available from craft and decorating stores), following the manufacturer's instructions, and fill the container so that it will cover the starfish by 1cm (½in). Press the starfish down into the mould-making material and leave to set. Remove the starfish when the mould is firm to the touch.

2 Following the manufacturer's instructions, mix up the plaster of paris in a glass jar and pour into the starfish shape. Leave to set, then very carefully release the starfish from the mould, bending it away from you as you go. It is likely to be very fragile so handle with care. Leave to dry for a few days and then paint both sides with two coats of emulsion paint. Finally, attach the motifs to the wall using adhesive pads.

Mediterranean magic

This **Mediterranean-style** bathroom, with its **marine blue** walls and **sea-inspired** decorations, instills an immediate **feeling of calm** and **tranquillity**.

Blue emulsion walls with a colourwash of turquoise paint, diluted with three parts water, and cream satin woodwork provide just the right background hues (use a long dry brush or a graining tool, available from do-it-yourself stores, for colourwashing.) The wavy fabric edge attached to the roller blind, the rope-framed mirror (see pages 68–9 for how to make the starfish) and seashell pictures combine to capture the essence of the Mediterranean.

You will need

circular or oval mirror
piece of plywood
mirror mastic
rope
craft adhesive
moulded starfish

1 Centre the mirror on the plywood (the wood should be at least 5cm/2in larger all round than the mirror) and fix it with mastic. Cut one tip of the rope at an angle so that it tapers neatly into the next piece when you coil it around. Apply adhesive to the plywood to secure the rope.

2 Wrap the rope around the mirror, remembering to cut the end tip at an angle. Leave to dry. Apply craft adhesive to the back of each starfish, and also to the rope.

3 Press each starfish into position and leave to dry before hanging the mirror on the wall with strong screw hooks and picture wire.

Taking its cue from the peaceful waters of the Mediterranean, this bright, sunny bathroom is a relaxing retreat.

display tips

A picture rail or high-level shelf is a safe, splash-free zone for bathroom ornaments, such as shell collections and coloured glass bottles. Instead of pictures on the wall, which may wrinkle in a damp bathroom, why not make your own original works of art with patterns of mosaic tiles?

Tiles with style

You don't have to be a **budding Rembrandt** to try your hand at painting. With **ceramic paints**, you can easily create your own **unique** tiles – try one of these designs or **invent your own**.

There are times when you are ready for a change but don't want to get involved in major redecorating, which can cost the earth. One easy way to brighten up a kitchen or bathroom is to hand-decorate plain ceramic tiles. Ceramic paints are as versatile as poster colour, so you can use them for all sorts of different effects such as sponging and stencilling, as well as for freehand designs. For strong impact, keep your designs simple, and aim for a stylized effect rather than a naturalistic one. You might want to use a motif that relates to the purpose or theme of the room – knives, forks and spoons in a kitchen; fish, boats or shells in a bathroom – or pick up a pattern or colour already used in the room, such as on the wallpaper, curtain fabric or decorative frieze.

If you are working directly on a tiled wall or splashback, it is worth trying out your design on a spare, loose tile first. As well as enabling you to check the effect, this gives you a chance to get the feel of working with ceramic paint. Draw inspiration from things around you – look for abstract shapes as well as actual objects. You can try leaves or flowers, kitchen objects such as salt and pepper mills, cups and saucers, kettles, or perhaps your pets – a cat, a goldfish, maybe even a mouse! If you want to sketch out your design before painting it, use a Chinagraph pencil, which works well on the shiny surface. Follow your sketch with ceramic paint outliner and leave it to dry before erasing the pencil guide.

Tiles hand painted with colourful stylized fish and decorated border pattern tiles are just right for a bathroom. The wiggly lines of the border pattern are painted in a shimmering gold.

paint facts

There are various types of ceramic paints available from art and craft shops. The ones used here can be fired in an ordinary oven for 35 minutes at 150–160°C (300–325°F), or set with the heat of a hairdryer. If you plan to decorate tiles that are already fixed in place, make sure you choose paints like these that can be set with a hairdryer. Always follow the manufacturer's instructions.

Stencilling tiles

Design your own stencil for ceramic tiles or use one from our selection of motifs on pages 136–7. You can enlarge or reduce these images on a photocopier.

※ If your tiles are already fixed to the wall, wipe them clean with white spirit to remove any traces of dust or grease before painting or stencilling.

※ Lay the stencil on the tile, taping it lightly to hold it in place. Using a paintbrush or small sponge, apply the ceramic paint, then carefully remove the stencil.

Decorate your kitchen tiles with knives, forks and spoons. You can even continue the pattern on inexpensive white china.

Custom made

Gone are the days when shelves were purely **functional**. Customize basic shelves to turn them into a **feature** to be proud of with **decorative** detailing and **innovative** ideas.

This simple shelf unit has been given a full makeover. A square of imitation silver leaf is stuck to the backboard, with bas-relief interest from a plaster heart and star, both sprayed silver.

It's so quick and easy to transform a plain wall with a shelf or pair of matching shelves which are both useful and ornamental. Inexpensive, basic shelves are readily available from do-it-yourself and home furnishings stores, or you can simply make your own from planed timber or MDF (particleboard), and then customize them to complement your room. Brackets can be plain and unobtrusive or a decorative element in their own right; you can make a template to your own design in thin card, then cut brackets from sawn timber with an electric jigsaw.

Edgings are another way to create very different effects – precut edging can be fixed to a shelf pelmet-style below the edge or with the decoration pointing upwards, making an attractive display shelf for china (see far right).

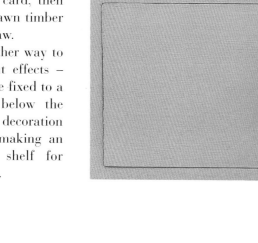

customized shelving

• Buy precut glass shelving, which has a rounded, polished edge, and etch a simple pattern or motif into it with etching paste (available from craft suppliers).

• Give plain shelves a touch of class with grooved beading fixed to the front edge.

• Support metal cooling trays on steel brackets for contemporary shelving suitable for a kitchen, bathroom or home office.

• Brighten up a budget, self-assembly shelf unit by painting the rear inside wall of the shelves in a dark colour and the shelves in a contrasting lighter shade or paler tint of the same colour to make an emphatic frame for china or ornaments.

This shelf (left) is composed of a plain board which has had a groove routed out to accommodate a precut shelf trim. The shelf, trim and supporting brackets are painted a soft purple, complementing the beakers, for a neat finish.

A planed softwood shelf is turned into a pretty plate rack (right) with an MDF (particleboard) trim, which can also be used the other way up to form a pelmet-style edging. The trim is painted white so as not to detract from the delicate pierced china.

Buy small display shelves or make your own from softwood or MDF (particleboard), glass or metal. This type of small shelf is primarily ornamental and doesn't require the same strength of support and fixing as more substantial, functional shelving. Try using a pair of shelves for a striking wall feature or two corner shelves, one above the other. Use them to display a favourite ornament or piece of china, a beautiful shell or trailing houseplant, or even empty to complement a decorative moulding.

Back-stencilling a display shelf

You will need

thin card
masking tape
metallic spray paint

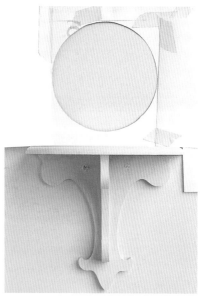

1 Cut out a stencil from thin card. Keep the shape simple – a circle, as shown here, or a diamond, star, heart or perhaps a stylized leaf (see pages 136–7). Tape the stencil to the wall with masking tape and protect the surrounding wall with paper, if necessary.

2 Use metallic decorative spray paint to spray silver in an even layer across the surface. Leave to dry briefly before removing the stencil. Add glass or silver accessories to complete the effect.

A simple display shelf steals the spotlight with the aid of a decorative paint effect (above). The shelves were painted a deeper blue than the wall behind, then a dramatic silver moon-like disc added above each one to create a sparkling 'halo' behind gleaming glassware filled with silvered almonds.

The same basic shelf is given a completely
different treatment with this dressy, theatrical
approach. A gold tassel is lightly tacked in
place to hang from the front of the shelf.
Alternatively, you can edge the shelf with
fringing or decorative furnishing braid.

Two types of gilt decoration are combined
to lend an opulent touch to the same type
of wall shelf (above). An imitation gold leaf
square was transferred onto the wall, then
a gilt plaster flower fixed in its centre. The
shelf was painted with the same paint as the
wall so that attention is drawn to its elegant
contours rather than its colour.

Wonderful windows

Wise up to **window style** and lift panes of glass into a **new dimension** with imaginative ideas coupled with a **touch of grandeur**…

When you enter a room, your gaze is naturally drawn towards the light, so make sure your windows are worth watching. Even a dull window can be dressed up into a splendid focal point with the right curtains or blind (for plenty of ideas, see pages 92–115). In this room, far right, the window seemed rather small in relation to the overall proportions, so it was dressed with floor-length curtains to give it more importance. Using a tabbed heading rather than a conventional gathered one also lends it greater emphasis. The window was crowned with a display shelf painted to match the sill trim. As well as providing space for pot plants or ornaments, this has the effect of apparently lengthening the proportions of the window area.

Instead of a soft, fabric pelmet, consider topping a window with a hard pelmet made of timber or plywood. Pre-cut pelmets are usually available from home-decorating stores in a range of shapes that you can paint yourself or cut your own – first, measure the window and make a template in thin card. Try the template above the window before you cut the pelmet to check you are happy with the proportions and overall effect.

A shaped wooden pelmet has been given a theatrical touch with gold resin tassels fixed to each scallop (above). As an alternative, stick a simple decorative moulding such as a star or semi-sphere along the pelmet at regular intervals.

Coordinated paintwork and careful detailing combine to turn a simple window into a stunning feature (right). Painting separate elements in the same shade helps to create a cohesive scheme. Simple pots add an unforced charm.

Recapture an age of classical splendour with this sumptuous, pre-cut pediment adorned with a gold-painted laurel wreath (left). You can make a decorative garland using wired artificial or dried foliage, then spray it with metallic paint.

Special effects

You don't need to be **clever at crafts** to create stylish and **original looks**. With **stick-on** accessories, you can **transform** the dull into the **divine**.

If you like the idea of carved or relief details but think you need to be an artist to incorporate them in your furnishings, think again. There is now an ever-increasing range of special accessories, architectural details, shapes and mouldings available from do-it-yourself and specialist decorating stores – which makes it easier to include them in all kinds of decorative schemes. A simple bathroom cabinet (see right) was turned into an elegant asset for a bathroom combining classical style with a coastal theme. The original doorknob was removed and replaced with a starfish-shaped handle echoed by silver-painted stars. To pick up the seaside details used elsewhere in the room, a few seashells were drilled and threaded onto cord for an informal, decorative touch.

   In a room of high ceilings and urbane sophistication, decorative corbels – which look like small pillar tops – set a classical tone. Playing with the theme of antiquity, these corbels have been used in conjunction with blocks that have a faux crackle effect. You can create a similar effect by making a crackle glaze to emulate an aged veneer. Genuine crackle is applied between two layers of paint so that the top one cracks in places, allowing the one beneath to show through. Stencils are also available to let you fake the effect.

These plaster corbels (right) may be left plain white or painted to complement the surrounding colour scheme. Use them to display a favourite ornament or vase containing a single, perfect bloom.

A simple wooden cupboard has been given a new look by being repainted and its old handle swapped for an ornamental one (below). If you have a completely plain cabinet, try reviving it with a decorative shelf trim at the base, wooden moulding at the top and beading to create a panelled door.

Stuck-on style

Why limit yourself to redecorating in only two dimensions? With a range of stick-on **period details** and **classic** shapes, you can enter the **third dimension**…

devoted to details

If you have a boring, boxy room to decorate that is devoid of interesting alcoves or original architectural details, consider using prefabricated mouldings to provide textural interest. This might be anything from a simple dado rail, perhaps dividing darker paintwork below with a lighter tone above, to ornate cornicing with a central ceiling rose and wooden panelling.

Perfect accessories for the instant decorator, mouldings, trims, shapes and salvaged beachcombing finds such as shells and interesting fragments of driftwood provide plenty of ideas for ways to spice up a tired or out-of-date scheme.

A decidedly sumptuous feel is created by this classic combination of barleytwist moulding (see below), used to make a panelled effect, with a gilt plaster star and semi-spheres. These are available from specialist decorating stores, or you can make your own decorative shapes from craft clay, which will set hard in an ordinary domestic oven.

Plain plaster or wooden shapes may be given a sophisticated twist by being sprayed with metallic paint. For a children's room, look out for small wooden or plastic toys that can be sprayed and fixed to the wall or as handles for a cupboard.

This plain wooden clock was given a completely new look by being lightly sanded to provide a 'key' for the paint, then painted in a soft wedgwood blue colour. Cockle shells discovered on the beach were painted silver and fixed with strong glue, with small plaster shells used for the top arch.

A picture rail adds architectural interest and makes unsightly nail holes a problem of the past. As well as plain and grooved styles, there are also exquisitely decorated picture rails available, like this one. Draw attention to the feature by using bright silver or brass picture hooks and pretty chain rather than ordinary picture cord.

MACULATA SHELL

CONSTRUCTION & COLOURATION AUG 1 1893

Classical details

Introduce a touch of **classical splendour** and **timeless style** to your home with ready-made mouldings and **ornamental** casts in a **rich array** of designs.

The natural beauty of a seashell is captured in this plaster plaque, which makes an unusual feature in a classical or maritime themed bathroom (see pages 22–3, 26–9).

A gothic arch shape is the inspiration for this painted moulding (top). Such mouldings may be used as a cornice or dado rail. Alternatively, a short length can serve as a pelmet above a window or either way up as a shelf trim.

A ready-cut pelmet is given an additional dimension with a plaster fleur-de-lys (above), a treatment that will work well for a large window. Both pelmet and plaster motif may be painted to coordinate with the curtains or the room's colour scheme.

In the right setting, even a more elaborate piece (left) need not look out of place. Use highly ornamental plaster mouldings like these with restraint, or they will lose their natural elegance.

Moulded to perfection

Ornamental details such as **mouldings**, carved accessories, **edge trims**, decorative **panels** and plaster **plaques** give **new dimensions** to featureless rooms.

Dado rails, corbels, trims and plaques can transform even the plainest room or hallway into an elegant space. These architectural details are generally easy to glue or nail into place, so are ideal if you want to make a dramatic change but are short of time. Available in an enormous range of styles, shapes and finishes, mouldings and trims can add a decorative finish to both classic and contemporary settings.

Traditionally, these details were usually moulded in plaster or carved from wood. Some are still made in this way, but mouldings have entered the modern age and many are now sold preformed from plastic. These have the undeniable advantages of being lightweight, inexpensive and easy to clean.

Turn a plain wall into a talking point with moulded plaster blocks like these (above). Small blocks are used in two rows to form a striking open frame for the ornate iris plaque in the centre.

For a room where you want something extra special and a little out of the ordinary, try hand-carved wooden mouldings such as this one (left). You can use a small length to crown a doorway or run above a fireplace.

in glorious colour

You may well want to leave any mouldings or trims plain white for a classical look, but don't forget that plaster and wooden details can also be painted. Pick out details in a single colour or with touches of silver, gold or bronze paint, or treat the entire area with paint or colourwash.

This classical-style hallway has been elaborately decorated with a mixture of ornamental edgings and wallpapers (left). The bas-relief carved effect has been achieved in the shaped panels with a textured wallpaper.

Combining two types of beading, rail or edge trim is one way to create a panelled effect on a wall or wardrobe or cupboard doors (above). A wheatsheaf moulding and flower squares have also been incorporated into the design.

Style on a shoestring

You don't have to be a millionaire to **create** a home that others **envy**. Forget about flash furnishings and overpriced trimmings – go for **clever detailing** with a little **know-how** and a **touch of flair**...

A fragment of wallpaper takes on new emphasis when it is bordered by a well-proportioned frame (right). You can also try out this idea with a piece of fabric, an old book jacket, even a section of giftwrapping paper.

Plain ceramic tiles pick out complementary colours from elsewhere in the room and create an emphatic border between the wallpaper and colourwash (below). For traditional and old-style bathroom fittings, check out architectural salvage companies, auctions and junk shops or garage sales.

When decorating a room, it's all too easy to focus on the large areas – walls, floor, curtains – and overlook the details. But stylish and interesting details are key ingredients of a harmonious and attractive home. Although some accessories and detailing may be added once you have completed the basic decorating, other elements are best planned at the very beginning as part of the overall scheme.

In a bathroom or kitchen, fancy patterned ceramic tiles can add enormously to decorating costs, and also tie you down to a particular look. Plain tiles often look as good as patterned ones – or even better – and offer much more versatility. In this bathroom, a tiled border was made between a wallpapered lower part and painted upper part, using tiles in three different colours mixed randomly for an informal and eye-catching effect (see box, far right, for more innovative ideas on what to do with plain tiles).

in the frame

Don't forget the importance of having the right frame. A good frame can turn even the most ordinary image into something special. The style should relate in some way to the decorating scheme or theme of the room.

• Buy cheap, raw wood frames and paint, stain or decorate them yourself.

• Make a frame from driftwood – this is ideal for a maritime picture or to frame a shell or model boat.

• For a contemporary look, enliven an old frame with metallic spray paint.

• Decorate a frame with small shells fixed with tile adhesive or strong glue.

• Stick on small beads or buttons for a colourful and encrusted effect.

• Make a frame from lengths of rope secured together (see page 70).

• Make your own mosaic frame from pieces of old china or ceramic tiles.

on the tiles

Try some of these ideas for using plain ceramic tiles.

• Continue a splashback up and around a plain fixed wall mirror to provide it with a matching frame.

• Fix tiles diagonally rather than square on, so that they make a diamond shape (see pages 22–3).

• Make a simple pattern with two or three colours of plain tiles, such as chequerboard, alternating stripes of colours or a broad band edged by a contrasting shade.

• Add your own painted, stencilled or relief design using ceramic paints (see pages 29 and 72–3).

• Add some pigment, such as acrylic paint, to the grouting to tint it a contrasting or complementary colour.

Sometimes the right picture can really make a room. Keep an open mind about sources of interesting images and objects for framing. As well as paintings, look out for low-budget pictures: posters, art prints and botanical engravings from second-hand or damaged books; even good-quality gift cards can look surprisingly effective with the right frame. Consider objects that can be displayed in a box frame, with a recessed back – look for attractive shells, a perfect pressed flower, a colourful toy car. Pictures kept permanently in a bathroom or small kitchen may suffer the effects of condensation – so hang your priceless Picasso elsewhere!

CURTAINS & BLINDS

Wise up to window style with elegant ideas for every room of the house, including easy-to-make blinds and no-sew curtains.

A matter of muslin

Most windows seem **underdressed** without some form of curtain. From **minimal sheers** to **luxurious toile de Jouy**, there is a window treatment for every type of room and **lifestyle**.

Proving that brilliant window dressing need not take hours of stitching, hemming and pleating, these gorgeous muslin curtains went up in one afternoon. They're unbelievably simple to make, with no sewing needed at all. Two lengths of the flimsy fabric in bright contrasting colours were just draped so that they hung evenly on both sides when swathed over a curtain pole. The front pieces were then crossed and drawn aside, and tied to the back sections in a loose knot.

Lightweight and translucent fabrics such as muslin, voile and organza make perfect curtains in rooms where privacy isn't a concern. They are also best reserved for the warmer months of the year: in winter, replace them with curtains in a heavier fabric, perhaps velvet or brocade, which are invaluable in preventing draughts and keeping in warmth.

A metal loop, originally designed for holding towels, has been screwed to the wall to make an unusual and distinctive tieback. This type of tieback can also be used with curtains of heavier fabric.

taking up the slack

Curtains tucked behind tiebacks form a graceful frame to any window. In their simplest form, tiebacks consist of a cord looped round the curtain and attached to a hook on the wall. Solid restraints such as wrought-iron tiebacks and brass rosettes are more sophisticated and look good with full, heavy curtains.

Raffia twisted in on itself and with the ends tied together behind the curtain makes a pretty tieback (above).

This window was given a simple yet elegant treatment by draping two pieces of muslin over a curtain pole and tying them together in a knot (right).

Turning the tables

The **ultimate** in ready-to-hang curtains, these **smart checked drapes** can be made in no time at all; all you need is a packet of **curtain clips** and a couple of **tablecloths**.

all tied up

Tied headings are one of the simplest ways of hanging lightweight curtains. Sew, or glue with fabric glue, ribbons to the tops of your curtains and tie them around the curtain pole. The ribbon may not slide that smoothly over the pole, so use such headings in rooms where the curtains are not opened and shut frequently.

These stylish and colourful curtains created from two ready-made cotton tablecloths are deceptively simple to make and hang. They're particularly appealing for anyone who dislikes sewing: the finished edges mean that no hemming is required. Too long for this particular window, the tablecloths were folded over at the top to create an instant pelmet.

As well as tablecloths, consider alternatives such as sheets, rugs, throws, bedspreads or blankets. Just make sure that whatever you choose is wide enough to hang in generous folds – nothing looks worse than skimpy curtains. Use curtain clips that slide onto the pole to grip the curtains in place. Finials prevent them from sliding off the pole when pulled.

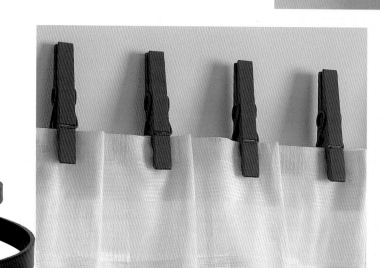

off the peg

Clothes pegs make inexpensive and innovative alternatives to standard curtain hooks. Perfect for voiles and other lightweight fabrics, the pegs clip onto curtain wire, making curtain hanging a quick and simple operation.

Whether corkscrews, curls or spearheads, wrought-iron finials (right) and poles are well suited to brightly coloured, contemporary fabrics.

Original and inexpensive, this stylish window treatment (right) combines a pair of cotton checked tablecloths with dramatic curtain clips and finials.

Starry nights

After a long day, **treat yourself** to a touch of **stardom**. Surround your bath or shower with these sumptuous **hand-dyed drapes** decorated with a **batik effect**.

If you want to give a bathroom a different look without redecorating the whole room, make a feature of the bath or shower with sweeping, canopy-style curtains that pool luxuriously onto the floor; they're quick and easy to make, and with simple curtain clips, take no time to hang. For these curtains, plain calico was used, dyed blue and stencilled with batik fluid to make a pattern of stars all over the fabric. If the curtain is to double as a shower curtain, either protect the dyed fabric with a waterproof lining, or hang a shower curtain on a second, inner rail concealed from view.

A similar idea can also be tried in a bedroom, using a circular canopy hoop set above the bed, with long falls of material framing the bed down to the floor. Leave the curtains loose or tie them back with heavy cord or a tieback made from the same fabric twisted or plaited into a decorative rope. For a lighter effect, you can use a sheer fabric such as muslin, perhaps stencilled with gold stars or printed with a rubber stamp motif (see pages 10–13).

a good match

Even if you're not planning to redecorate the entire room, try to pick up the curtain colour or star motif somewhere else in the room to tie it into the existing scheme – perhaps with star-shaped candle holders or a star-stencilled mirror frame, or choose towels or a floor mat in a similar shade of blue as the curtains.

Bathtime is lifted into the realm of luxury with batik-stencilled curtains suspended from a curtain canopy hoop. Simple curtain clips were used so there was no need to sew on curtain heading tape.

How to batik-dye fabric

For these curtains, a batik technique was used. For ease and convenience, a proprietary batik fluid rather than molten wax ensures that the star design remains uncoloured after the fabric has been dyed.

You will need

cardboard for template
scalpel or craft knife
5m (16ft) natural calico fabric
masking tape
small brush
batik fluid or wax
cold water dye
circular canopy hoop
curtain clips and rings

1 Trace a star shape onto the card and cut it out using a scalpel. Hold the stencil in place on the fabric with masking tape and brush on the wax liberally. Apply the stars randomly, or make a regular pattern: cut a square piece of card, turn it through 90 degrees to form a diamond and mark the four corners. Position stars at these points, then move the card down and repeat.

2 Allow the curtain fabric to dry thoroughly overnight. Place a piece of cloth over the curtain and iron to fix the design in place — make sure that the stars are protected as they are not heat-resistant. Prepare the cold water dye according to the instructions on the packet. Place the curtain in a large, flat container, with as few folds as possible, and add the dye solution.

3 When the dyeing process is complete, rinse the fabric well and leave it to dry. Centre the canopy rail above the bath, fixing the rail to brackets on the shelf and hang the curtains — clips were used here as a quick and easy, no-sew method of attaching the fabric to the rail.

Banner waving

No fuss, no frills – and almost no sewing. Dress up a window in very **little time** with this simple **banner-style** pelmet made from a fabric panel tied in place onto wooden **doorknobs**.

This fabric banner is a great idea for brightening up a room quickly without embarking on a major project. Just a simple panel of fabric tied across the top of the window, it is also a novel way to show off a bold pattern or make the most of an expensive remnant. You can even use a fabric you have decorated yourself with fabric paint or dye, perhaps printed with a rubber stamp or patterned with a stencil.

To attach the pelmet to the wall, use curtain tiebacks, doorknobs or drawer knobs – you can buy unfinished wooden ones and then paint or spray them to match your decorating scheme. If wooden doorknobs would look out of place in your room, look out for those made of brass, iron or crystal-effect cut glass instead.

1 Cut out a rectangle of fabric 10cm (4in) wider than the distance between the outer doorknobs. Hem the fabric on all sides using iron-on hemming tape.

2 Make a pleat at the top of either end of the fabric and pin in place. Make a double pleat in the centre of the panel and pin.

fixed ideas

An entire curtain can also be hung at the window from this type of fixing. Lightweight materials, such as cottons and sheers, produce the best effect because heavy curtains tend to drag and so spoil the overall appearance. Try using different materials for the bows: for instance, wide satin or velvet ribbon can add a romantic touch to a bedroom.

How to make a banner-style pelmet

First, mark the position of the doorknobs: one should be in the centre and one on either side of the window frame. Attach them securely to the wall using wall plugs and double-ended screws.

You will need

wooden drawer knobs

wall plugs

double-ended screws

curtain fabric

iron-on hemming tape

3 Fold three 30cm (12in) lengths of hemming tape, ribbon or matching cord in half lengthways and sew each one behind a pleat. Tie to the doorknobs.

For this banner-style pelmet, a bold fabric with a postcard design was used, conjuring up a theme of exotic locations and lazy days that was continued with the model lighthouse and starfish.

Heading for the top

You don't have to be elaborate to be **elegant**. This soft pelmet uses **minimal** fabric to match the curtains and provide an **effective frame** for the window.

full folds

If you want very full, opulent curtains or are using a heading tape with a pinch pleat or pencil pleat style, your overall fabric width should measure at least twice the length of the pole – 1½ times the length will make gentler folds suitable for curtains with a standard gathered heading.

This simple fabric pelmet manges to look dressy without being over-formal. No special equipment is needed as no stiffening or boards are used, and very little sewing is involved. Consequently, this pelmet takes very little time to make.

The easy style looks equally good in a traditional or modern setting, at home in a townhouse or country cottage. If you have an existing curtain, adding this type of pelmet on a lightweight pole is a clever way to disguise a plain curtain track. You can use a patterned fabric for the pelmet with plain curtains to draw greater attention to the pelmet and make it a more striking feature.

Choose a curtain pole that has brackets deep enough to keep the pelmet well away from the curtains behind, so that it doesn't become snagged up when you draw the curtains. For a generous look, make sure that the pelmet measures at least a fifth of the overall curtain length.

Softer yet more emphatic than plain curtains with no heading, this gently gathered fabric pelmet frames a well-proportioned window, drawing you towards an attractive view outside.

How to make the pelmet

You will need
curtain fabric
iron-on hemming tape
curtain pole

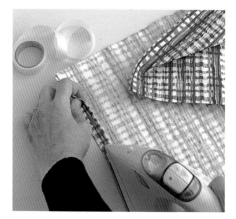

1 Hem the sides and lower edge of the fabric using iron-on tape.

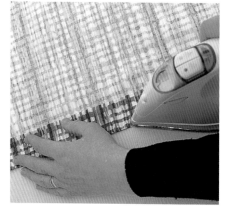

2 Make a turning along the top edge deep enough to contain the pole and press. For a tight fit, first add 5mm (¼in) to the diameter of the pole. Divide this measurement in half to get the distance of the sewing line from the fold.

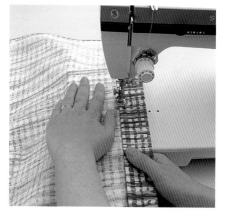

3 Stitch the turning in place along the top of the pelmet to make a tube. Slot the pole through and hang.

If you like the look and feel of muslin but are concerned that it doesn't offer enough privacy, you can fit a roller blind in the same shade as the curtain. Discreet when rolled up, the blind can be pulled down behind the muslin for complete privacy as and when required.

Eastern promise

Soft and **feminine**, reminiscent of an Eastern palace, these **exotic** pink muslin curtains are a **quick** and **easy** way of **revitalizing** a tired decorating scheme.

Muslin hanging at the window will, after time, start to yellow, but there's no need to invest in new curtains. Instead, dyeing the fabric a colour to complement the room will give your curtains a completely new lease of life. Here, the muslin has been hand-dyed in three stages to create an unusual graduated colour design.

to dye for

There are various ways to dye or decorate muslin for drapes, canopies and hangings: try wax-resist techniques such as batik, tie-dye, stencilling or stamping. Use falls of muslin at windows to filter the light, on a canopy hoop as a luxurious addition over a bed or bath, stretched or pleated across a frame to make a translucent screen, or hanging from a pole behind a bed – loose or softly gathered.

Fluttering gently in the breeze, these romantic muslin curtains are the perfect window dressing for a sunny downstairs room leading out into the garden.

Hand-dyeing in graduated colours

By dipping sections of the muslin in the dye for different lengths of time, you achieve a pretty and unusual gradation of colour.

You will need
length of muslin
safety pins
washing-up bowl
hand dye
rubber gloves

Preparation
Wash and dry the muslin. Attach safety pins across the cloth in lines to mark three sections. Make sure the muslin fits into the bowl. If it is too wide, fold it in half lengthways. Wet the fabric thoroughly and squeeze out any excess water.

1 Make up the dye according to the instructions on the packet. (Always remember to wear rubber gloves when working with dye.) Immerse the muslin in the dye solution to the first line of safety pins and gently agitate the submerged section. After 17 minutes, feed in the second section and agitate.

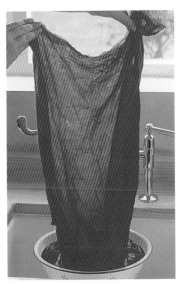

2 After a further 17 minutes, add the last section and agitate for nine minutes. Rinse in cold water, according to the instructions, remove the pins and wash in a machine at the temperature stipulated.

103

Sprightly sprigs

Create a **coordinated** look for stylish windows with these light, tabbed **floral curtains** and an ingenious **double-sided** blind.

In a room with one large window and a second, smaller one, it might look too fussy to have sweeping drapes at both windows. One approach might be to frame the principal window with curtains, then use the same fabric to make a neat blind for the other window. If you want a dressier effect, use both curtains and blind together – the blind also acts as insulation to keep in the heat.

For this blind, two different fabrics were used for a double-sided effect, providing a contrasting edge. Neutral hessian (burlap) provides textural interest, but you can also use a plain cloth in a shade that picks up one of the colours from the patterned fabric.

twice as nice

To make the double-sided blind, choose two different but complementary fabrics.

1 First measure the window, adding a 2.5cm (1in) seam allowance on either side. Cut out a piece of each of the two types of fabric to this measurement.

2 With right sides facing, stitch the two pieces together along three sides, then turn them the right side out and hand sew the last edge.

3 Insert a row of eyelet holes down each side. Gather the fabric into thick folds and mark the position of the eyelet hole in the centre of each fold. Fix eyelets in place and thread cord through, knotting at the bottom so that the blind pulls up into deep, concertina-style folds.

An elegant metal curtain pole and matching metal holdbacks add a touch of sophistication to a pair of unpretentious floral print curtains (above). At the same window, a blind made of identical fabric lined with hessian (burlap) creates a completely different look (left).

Making waves

Strike a **contemporary** note with this **no-frills** pelmet to match your roller blind. For this **extremely easy** project, you don't even need a good eye to **get it right**!

Making a matching pelmet for your blind couldn't be simpler with the aid of a pelmet stiffener kit, available from good soft furnishings suppliers or department stores. The kits come with a paper backing marked with a grid and pre-drawn shapes for the edging. The adhesive surface keeps the fabric smooth and you can fix it directly to the architrave around the window or to a pelmet shelf. Use fabric glue to add decorations, such as ribbon and buttons or an edging trim.

customized trim

A plain pull-down blind can be easily customized with a fabric trimming. Although only minimal sewing skills are required, there are companies that specialize in custom-trimming blinds. Consult your curtains and blinds supplier.

A matching pelmet gives a more formal and finished appearance to this bedroom window, as well as helping to prevent draughts.

Creating a shaped pelmet

You will need
fabric
pelmet stiffener
fabric glue
Velcro

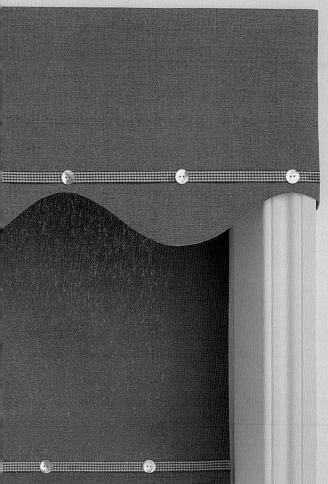

1 Measure the width and depth of the architrave, and cut out the pelmet stiffener to fit your chosen shape. Cut out fabric that is 5cm (2in) larger all round.

2 Cut away the backing paper to reveal the sticky surface. Match up the centre of the fabric and press together. Remove the paper and smooth the fabric onto the surface. Trim the fabric to leave a 1cm (½in) allowance and cut notches round the curved edge so the fabric turns neatly.

3 Glue the notched fabric in place (for neatness you can glue on a piece of backing fabric). Attach Velcro to the architrave and the top edge of the pelmet. Press together.

Level pegging

Instead of a curtain track, use a **Shaker-style** peg rail for a fabric-tabbed blind. **Easy to hang** and take down for washing, the bright checked panel is bound with a green braid to make **fuss-free** window dressing.

poles & pipes

Instead of a peg rail, use an inexpensive wooden broom handle for a rustic look. Stain or paint the pole to complement the fabric and support it with brackets or hooks. For a more modern look, use copper or chrome pipe, available from plumbers' merchants, with bold, plain or patterned fabric.

Perfect for masking an unsightly view, this blind, made from a rectangle of checked fabric and edged with contrasting braid, hangs from a wooden peg rail.

The neat fabric loops along the top edge of this blind are tailor-made for hanging on a wooden peg rail. During the day, the fabric can be drawn to the side and looped over a hook to let in the light. Alternatively, you can attach loops to the bottom corners to allow the blind to be folded in half upwards and then hung over the pegs.

To make the blind, cut a piece of fabric slightly larger than your window, plus an 8cm (3in) wide contrasting edging for all four sides and enough 20cm (8in) long pieces of fabric for the loops. Attach the edging with iron-on hemming tape, then attach the loops by folding them in half and sewing along the top of the blind at intervals to correspond with the pegs.

As an alternative to fabric tabs, you can use painted wooden curtain rings, which will slot neatly over the row of pegs. If you don't want to fix a peg rail, a row of decorative metal hooks will make another good hold-up.

This style of blind can be hung in a number of different ways. Here, curtain rings slip over a Shaker-style peg rail (right, above), while fabric tabs hang from the same peg rail (main picture) or from decorative metal hooks (right, below).

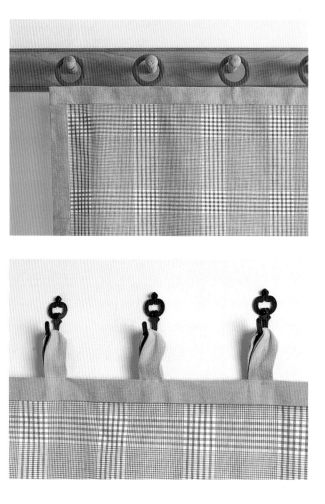

Brilliant blinds

Simple and **fast to make**, with the **minimum of sewing**, these two blinds are perfect for **brightening** up a small bathroom window.

These two styles of blind are both easy to make in a short session. Either is ideal for a small window, perhaps in a hallway, cloakroom or landing, or for a study or attic bedroom. For the check blind, a neat alternative to heading tape was used in the form of ribbon loops spaced at intervals, which were hung on decorative hooks. The ribbon-tied blind has the simplest possible heading: sticky-backed Velcro, with one part stuck to the blind and the other onto the wall, which works well for a lightweight fabric.

If making a static blind – to be kept half-open – gather it up in loose folds and secure it in place; if you need to raise and lower the blind, add a length of Roman blind tape on the reverse of the fabric, a third of the way in from each side hem.

This small window has been made into more of a feature by painting the frame in a colour that coordinates with the blind.

1 First, measure the window and cut out a panel of your chosen fabric, allowing enough overlap all round for the hem. Then hem the fabric so that it's slightly larger than the window.

2 Cut two lengths of ribbon, each measuring twice the drop of the blind. Stitch the two ribbons halfway along their length to the top of the blind, so that half hangs in front of the blind and half behind it.

3 Attach the blind to the window frame with sticky-backed Velcro – this makes it easy to remove for cleaning. Gather up the fabric and tie the ribbons into bows underneath to hold it in place.

Let there be light

Let in the light with these **translucent** treatments – a Roman blind **edged with lace,** a basic **gingham** pelmet and a **swathe** of elegant muslin.

Where it's important to maximize light levels, keep curtains and blinds light and simple. Look out for translucent fabrics such as muslins, lace, organza, voile or net; loose-woven linen or hessian may be preferable if you need something more substantial. A single length of muslin, fixed to the wall with double-sided tape, makes a beautiful instant pelmet (see right). If you are using a heavier fabric, you should first fix it to a batten, which is then screwed to the wall. To maintain a light effect, but ensure greater privacy, you can combine two or more layers of sheer fabric, such as lace and muslin.

A window with just a plain blind may look rather bare. To dress it up, add a gathered pelmet. The one shown here (see far right) is easy to make in a matter of minutes. Cut and hem the fabric to the correct depth and gather it into soft folds. Then, sew Velcro along the top edge and glue or staple the matching Velcro along the top of the window frame.

This simple swagged heading is a good way of exploiting the quality of a sheer material (above). Try it with plain, stencilled or dyed muslin or even a synthetic lace or net.

A plain cream Roman blind is keyed in to the colour scheme of this hallway with a pelmet headed in a lightweight gingham fabric, which lets in the light (right).

on the edge

Customize a plain blind with your own edging. With the Roman blind here (right), cream lace was attached along the bottom edge before hanging in place. For a no-sew method, use iron-on hemming tape instead. If lace doesn't suit the style of the room, try a narrow edging band of fabric to coordinate with the pelmet, or ribbon, upholstery braid or fringing.

A delicate, textured effect is created by trimming an ordinary calico blind with a strip of hemmed lace (above) – a good way of using up an odd remnant left over from a lace curtain used elsewhere.

Tying the knot

Coordinating curtains and blinds help unify the decorating scheme of a room. **Thick rope** holding up a colourful blind and a bath curtain in the same fabric continue the **tropical, maritime** theme established in this **Caribbean-style** bathroom.

keeping dry

Whether made from fabric or plastic, blinds are particularly practical in bathrooms where they can be hoisted up away from damp surfaces. If you choose wooden, slatted blinds, make sure they are suitable for bathroom use and able to withstand the effects of damp and condensation.

Simple and fun, these coordinating window blinds and bath curtain in a brightly patterned fabric (right) give this bathroom a vibrant Caribbean feel.

Natural coir rope tied in a knot (below) is a decorative as well as practical way of holding up these attractive bathroom blinds.

Forget sophisticated manufactured blinds and make your own with the fabric of your choice and natural coir rope. First, cut and hem the fabric to the correct size. Sew Velcro along the top edge and staple or stick the rest of the Velcro along the top of the window frame. Secure the blind in place. Cut two lengths of rope twice the length of the blind (you can trim this later if necessary).

Fold both lengths of rope in half and staple the centre of each piece to the top of the window recess (make sure they are spaced evenly apart), leaving two lengths hanging, one behind the fabric and one in front. Gather up the fabric to the required height and tie each of the lengths of rope together with a big knot. Adjust the fabric so that it swags in the centre.

If your budget doesn't run to a new bathroom suite, why not disguise a bath panel with a curtain to match the window blind? All you need do is cut and hem the fabric to the height of the bath panel by 2½ times the length. Then, stitch a length of press-on curtain tape to the top edge of the fabric and gather up. Stick matching grip tape to the top edge of the bath panel and press the fabric in place.

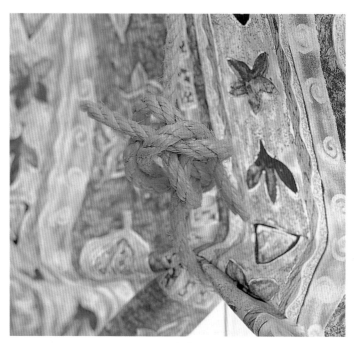

SOFT FURNISHINGS

Add comfort and coordination to any decorating scheme with simple, stylish cushions and throws and traditional covered screens.

Clever covering

The **folding screen** has been popular for centuries – and no wonder. Use one to create a feeling of **intimacy** or to **conceal** a utilitarian area. You can easily cover a screen to **tie in** with your **colour scheme**.

In these days of multi-purpose rooms, the traditional folding screen is making something of a comeback. Ideal for masking a dressing area in a bedroom or hiding away a home office or study corner in a sitting-room, a screen allows you to delineate the separate functions of an area without compromising on space or altering the room's natural proportions. Keep an eye out for damaged or marked screens at auction rooms, second-hand stores and sales. It is easy to rejuvenate a screen by recovering it with new fabric so that it complements the decorating scheme of the room.

For this screen, a neutral hessian (burlap) fabric was used for the covering. This kind of material is wonderfully versatile – vital if you plan to use the screen in different rooms at different times. It also provides a good background if you want to add a rubber-stamped motif (see page 13) or a stencilled pattern (see page 20).

fabrics for screens

Other fabrics suitable for covering screens include plain calico or sailcloth, or brightly coloured felt. For a more highly decorated finish, make a patch-work effect from fabric scraps or a découpage screen from a montage of cut-out pictures, photographs and designs from patterned papers.

How to cover a screen

You will need
folding screen
fabric for covering, such as
    hessian (burlap)
fabric adhesive
staple gun
decorative edging braid
brass-headed tacks

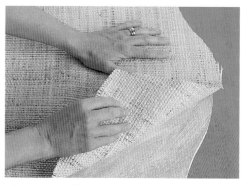

1 Remove the hinges from the screen to separate the panels. Cut the fabric to fit each panel, front and back, allowing enough for a 2cm (¾in) seam on all edges. Apply adhesive to one side of the panel and press on the hessian (burlap).

2 Stretching the fabric as you go, staple it in position along all the edges. Turn the panels over and repeat on the other side. Trim any excess or frayed edges.

3 Cover the top and side edges of each panel with braid, securing in place with decorative brass-headed tacks. Replace the hinges and join the panels together again to complete the screen.

In this bedroom, the folding screen conceals a small dressing area, providing privacy and hiding occasional clutter.

Customized cushions

Whether **plump** and filled with **feathers** or **flat** and filled with **foam**, cushions add **character** and **colour** to any room and seating arrangement.

terrific trimmings

It's easy to change the look of cushions with your own custom-made touches or trimmings, creating a different effect with the minimum of time, fuss or expense. Try some of the following:

• Add definition to cushions by edging them with contrasting piping.

• For a touch of baroque splendour, stitch on tassels to the corners of a square cushion or to either end of a bolster.

• Edge a cushion with upholstery braid or trimming, decorative thick cord or silk rope.

• Make a simple rosette from softly gathered or pleated fabric to attach to the centre of a round cushion.

• Add a pleated or gathered frill in the same fabric as the cushion cover, or a complementary colourway.

Two plain cushions have been transformed into attractive, customized soft furnishings: one, with an imprint of a favourite photograph, the other with a collection of brightly coloured contrasting buttons.

For the button cushion

You will need
fabric
button-covering kit
soft pencil

✳ Cut out small circles of fabric using guide supplied with the button-covering kit.

✳ Following the instructions supplied with the kit, fold the fabric around the button cover pushing it onto the 'teeth' and snap on the button back. Mark the position of the buttons on the cushion fabric with a soft pencil and then stitch them into place.

Buttons covered in a lively, red-checked fabric have given a simple cushion a distinctive facelift. A mixture of large and small buttons will create quite a different look.

For the photograph cushion

You can now buy easy-to-use image-making kits from crafts and soft furnishings suppliers that allow you to transfer photographs and pictures onto fabric.

You will need

pillowcase or cushion cover
fabric dye for background colour
piece of cardboard
white chalk pencil or stick of chalk
fabric paint in white and your choice
    of background colour
image-making kit
image to be lasercopied (at a photo-
    copying or photographic store)

Preparation

Dye a cushion cover or cotton pillowcase in your chosen colour, following the instructions on the packet. Then wash, dry and iron the cover.

1 Place a piece of cardboard inside the cushion cover and mark the shape of your chosen image in the middle of it with a white chalk pencil. Paint this area with white fabric paint. Leave the first coat to dry, fix with an iron and then apply a second coat. Leave to dry and iron again.

2 To use the image-making kit, follow the instructions supplied. Allow the image to dry overnight and then, using a damp cloth, gently rub the paper away until the image is exposed; you may need to do this a few times to remove the paper completely. When dry, paint a line round the picture with your background colour fabric paint to finish off. With your fingertip, rub a small amount of the image maker over the picture to seal it.

A favourite image has been imprinted onto a plain cushion. Remember, the picture on the fabric will be a mirror image of the original.

Stylish spiral

Enliven a jaded chair or sofa by draping it with a **striking throw** or bedspread that is **hand-dyed** then painted with an **artistic swirl** of colour.

For a really instant effect, cover up a dull or faded piece of furniture with a bright throw – perfect for disguising a battered old chair, enriching a folded screen or jazzing up a bed either as a cover or draped over the headboard. We gave a new lease of life to an old plain cream throw by dyeing it a warm sunshine yellow and painting it with a graphic spiral in a deep, contrasting colour.

There are fabric paints available in a wide range of colours, many of which are washable once they have been initially fixed. Refer to the packet guidelines to check how much dye you need for the weight of your throw and for fabrics suitable for dyeing. You can also try this idea with cushion covers, pillowcases or plain calico for curtains.

wise design

When it comes to conjuring up ideas for motifs and designs for painting on fabric, let your imagination go. Look for inspiration from strong shapes and patterns in objects around you. Opt for a stylized approach rather than a naturalistic one – it has more impact and is easier to carry out successfully even if you are a novice at painting.

How to dye and paint a throw

You will need

plain flat-weave throw or bedspread
cold water dye
cold fix
chalk or soft pencil
paintbrush
fabric paint

A wicker conservatory armchair that has partially faded in the sun has been given a fresh look with a vibrant yellow-dyed throw painted with a deep cinnamon spiral.

1 Wash the throw, then add the dye powder and cold fix to the washing machine drum, ensuring that the powder is evenly distributed. Add some salt, covering the area where the powder was added. Place the wet throw in the drum, and run a full 60°C (140°F) cycle (as for colour-fast cotton without pre-wash). Then add detergent and wash the throw on the longest, hottest wash recommended. If this has to be less than 95°C (200°F), remove the throw after the cycle is complete and then run a 95°C (200°F) programme with detergent to remove any dye from the machine.

2 If the throw's wash cycle was below 95°C (200°F), wash it separately a couple of times to remove excess dye. Leave it to dry away from direct heat and sunlight. First mark out your design on the fabric with chalk or a soft pencil. (Alternatively, use a stencil as the design template.) Using a paintbrush, apply the fabric paint to the throw. If the design is very complicated, try it out on paper first until you feel more confident.

Alphabet games

Add a **personal touch** of style with a **monogrammed cushion** or bolster bearing your initial in **decorative script** or bold letters – you can stencil one in **a matter of minutes!**

Lettering can be highly decorative – whether you use it to form actual words or phrases or as separate letters which throws more focus onto the shape of each individual letter. There are so many typefaces, from elegant, sloping scripts to chunky, modern capitals. Look in newspapers, magazines and books for examples of different styles, or use the choice of lettering at the back of this book (see pages 132–5).

Cutting out letters can be very fiddly, so it is better to use them as an under-template, where you trace over them rather than trying to cut around each one neatly. For this reason, use a pale, lightweight fabric such as muslin, poplin or light calico so that you can see the letter clearly beneath when you trace it. If you plan to make whole words, make sure you are happy with the letter spacing at the pencil-tracing stage before you start to paint the fabric.

see-through stencil

In some cases, it is easier to have a transparent stencil – for example, if you are composing words and need to see guidelines on the wall beneath. Make a stencil from a sheet of clear acetate (from art shops). Lay the acetate over the design, trace it off with a drawing pen, then cut out with a craft knife. Take care because the knife may slip on the smooth surface.

How to stencil lettering

Use a photocopier to enlarge or reduce the letter(s) you want to the right size.

You will need
letters to trace
lightweight pale fabric
pencil
plain paper
fabric paint
small paintbrush

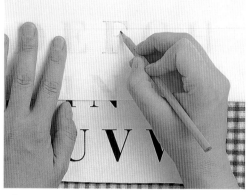

1 Copy the letter to the correct size to create a template, then cut your piece of fabric to size and lay it over the letter template, making sure it's correctly centred or aligned. Holding fabric and template in place, trace around the letter with a pencil.

2 Remove the letter template and rest the fabric on a sheet of plain paper (this makes the letter outline easier to see). Now fill it in using fabric paint and a small paintbrush.

3 If you are creating a repeated design or painting several letters, it's a good idea to outline a few of them first before you start filling them in, to get an idea of the general effect and correct any mistakes.

This impressive curtain, bolster and cushion were decorated by being hand-stencilled with individual script capital letters. Making the letters the same size creates a regular patterned effect, while varying the letter size, as on the bolster, puts more emphasis on each letter shape.

Finishing touches

This fabric lampshade (right) was decorated with burnt orange paint applied with a pre-cut rubber stamp. Alternatively, you can make your own stamp using foam rubber.

Give your decorating scheme that **extra special** something with your own choice of **creative flourishes** and accessories to add **individuality** and expression.

When you're decorating a room, don't forget the details. Paying attention to accessories and coordinating touches makes all the difference. These might be very simple – a ceramic bowl that picks up the colour of the curtains, scatter cushions to add colour and comfort – or they may involve a little more planning. There are no hard and fast rules about what works, so feel free to use your imagination or be a little experimental.

A simple idea that looks good in a bedroom or sitting-room is a decorated lamp, with the shade hand-stamped or stencilled to tie in with a design used elsewhere in the room, perhaps on the curtains or cushions. Try this on a side lamp or pendent ceiling shade. For this lamp, a rubber stamp was used to print a border around the lower edge of the shade. Reapply the paint freshly to the stamp each time for an even impression (see pages 10–13).

An easy idea to try if you're not keen on sewing is a beaded throw. Customize a plain fringed throw or bedspread with beads. Count along the fringe and, at every fifth length, join two together and thread on two or three beads. Knot to secure.

well drawn

A simple way to brighten up a bathroom is to use any leftover fabric from a curtain or blind to make coordinating accessories. We made a roomy drawstring bag that is perfect for storing all sorts of bathroom odds and ends, such as spare toilet rolls, make-up and toiletries, or as a laundry bag.

To make the bag, first cut the fabric to make a square, sew up the two open sides and turn inside out. Turn in an 8cm (3in) hem along the top of the bag and iron flat. Sew a line all the way around the bag 5cm (2in) from the top and another line 6.5cm (2½in) from the top, creating a channel for the cord to be threaded through.

Add a distinctive touch to an ordinary throw with beads threaded onto the fringe (right). Use ceramic, glass, wooden or hand-painted beads, or if you prefer something more lightweight, plastic beads which are available in gold and silver metallic finishes as well as a multitude of colours.

DECORATOR'S ESSENTIALS

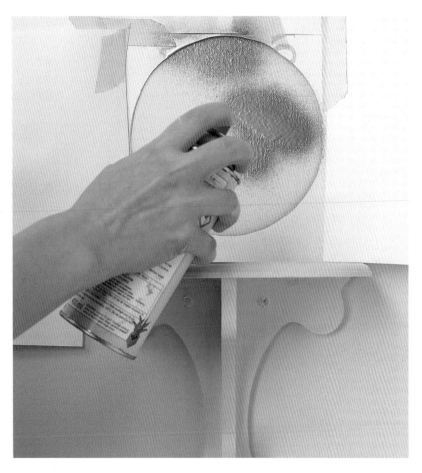

Everything the instant decorator needs to know, from practical tips, clever ideas and useful stockists to designs for decorative motifs and alphabets for your own stencils.

Practical pointers

These handy **hints**, key **reminders** and design **ideas** provide **inspiration** and useful **pointers** for speedy decorating, whether you're **revamping** an entire house or simply adding a few **finishing touches**.

✳ When trying out a new technique, tackle a small area first, or practise on a sample board until you're happy with the effect. This also helps you build your confidence.

✳ Think ahead: make sure you've got all the 'ingredients' the project needs before starting work so that you're not held up – some of the paint effects, in particular, need to be completed in one session.

✳ Avoid using oil-based gloss and eggshell paints unless they're specifically recommended for the project. Emulsion is generally easier to use, dries much faster and can be diluted with water for colourwashes and other effects. Oil-based paints are traditionally used on woodwork but emulsion often works just as well.

✳ Don't throw out old decorating materials that could be recycled for future projects. Leftover paint, spare tiles, fabric remnants and wallpaper offcuts can all be useful for sprucing up walls, furniture and fittings.

✳ Collect pictures of rooms and looks you like – postcards, pages from magazines. You don't have to copy the whole room, of course, but it's a good way of getting to know the colours and effects you enjoy living with.

the instant decorator's stock list

Some decorating 'ingredients' have a magical effect in creating instant impact. The following are essential items to keep in your decorating store cupboard – you never know when they'll come in handy.

• **Paint** Never throw tester pots away – one small pot should be enough to cover a chair or wall cabinet, and decorative patterns need only the smallest amount.

• **Calico & gingham** For pelmets, drapes, seat covers and drawstring bags. Calico is a good fabric background for stencil designs.

• **Rugs & throws** To transform chairs, sofas, beds and plain floors – or to adapt for layered curtain effects.

• **Cushions** Pile a random selection on sofas and beds to add extra comfort and colour.

• **Vases, jugs & other containers** Fresh flowers look good in almost anything, from a plain glass tank to a galvanized bucket – as long as the display is bold and confident, the container really doesn't matter.

• **Candles & candleholders** To create atmosphere and provide depth of lighting – a real fire does the same, but we're not all lucky enough to have one, so candles are the next best thing.

• **Decorative hooks** Great for hanging curtains or blinds, for display-ing dried flowers, wreaths or just utensils – they even look good with nothing hanging from them at all.

• **Baskets** For firewood, cutlery (silverware) and utensils, sewing mate-rials, make-up, correspondence, vegetables – you name it, it will almost certainly look better in a basket.

• **Tassels & trimmings** And all those delights you find in old-fashioned haberdashery (notions) departments – perfect for livening up window dressings, pelmets, cushions and chairs.

• **Buttons** They don't need to have a practical use, but they add a neat finish almost anywhere you fix them – use them to smarten up cushions and curtains or to decorate a plain lampshade.

Stencil designs

Use the **decorative alphabets** and **motifs** on the following pages for all kinds of projects – add a **monogram** to a cushion, plate or mug, **lettering** above a picture or dado rail or a **motif** such as a **leaf** or **heart** on a wall or floor.

To make a letter or motif into a stencil, first get it to the size you want using a photocopier. If working on a thin fabric, you can simply trace over the photocopied design. To make a template for use on ceramics or walls, lay the design over a sheet of carbon paper laid on top of a piece of stencil card and trace off the design. Remove the paper and carbon, and cut the card template following the transferred carbon outline.

Aa

Ee

IiJj

NnOoPp

UuVvWw

STOCKISTS & SUPPLIERS

Many of the general materials and supplies you may need can usually be found at good department stores or do-it-yourself outlets. For items relating to soft furnishings, such as fabrics and curtain fittings, look in curtain stores. Specialist supplies, such as ceramic paints, are better tracked down in art or craft stores. Some suppliers also have a mail order service; telephone the head office or principal outlet for details.

UNITED KINGDOM

PAINTS & WALLPAPERS

Crown Paints
PO Box 37
Hollins Road
Darwin
Lancashire BB3 0BG
01254 704951

Dulux
0891 515222 (colour advice)
01753 550555 (general)

Farrow & Ball
Uddens Trading Estate
Wimborne
Dorset BH21 7NL
01202 876141

Jane Churchill
151 Sloane Street
London SW1X 9BX
0171 730 9847 (shop)
0181 877 6400 (stockists)

John Oliver Paints
33 Pembridge Road
London W11 3HG
0171 221 6466

HARDWARE & DO-IT-YOURSELF

B&Q
0181 466 4166

Bombay Duck
 (decorative hooks)
231 The Vale
London W3 7QS
0181 749 8001 (mail order)

Clayton Munroe
 (handles, hooks, etc.)
Kingston West Drive
Staverton
Devon TQ9 6AR
01803 762626

Crofts & Assinder
 (knobs, fittings, etc.)
Lombard Street
Birmingham B12 0QX
0121 622 1074

Homebase
0645 801800

H & R Johnson Tiles
Highgate Tile Works
Brownhills Road
Stoke-on-Trent
Staffordshire ST6 4JX
01782 575575

James Mayor Furniture
 (doors)
160 Fazeley Street
Birmingham B5 5RS
0121 643 8344 (brochures)

Market Square Warminster
 (panelling, shelf poles)
Wing Farm
Longbridge Deverill
Warminster
Wiltshire BA12 7DD
01985 841041

Wickes Building Supplies Ltd.
120-38 Station Road
Harrow
Middlesex HA1 2QB
0500 300328

World's End Tiles
British Rail Yard
Silverthorne Road
London SW8 3HE
0171 819 2100

FABRIC, CURTAINS & BLINDS

Ametex Fabrics
Chiltern House
The Valley Centre
Gordon Road
High Wycombe
Buckinghamshire
HP13 6EQ
01494 474741

Clayton Munroe
see under Hardware

Dormy
Dormy House
Stirling Park
East Portway Industrial
 Estate
Andover
Hampshire SP10 3TZ
01264 365808
01264 365789 (brochures)

Harrison Drape
Customer Services
Bradford Street
Birmingham B12 0PE
0121 766 6111

Ian Mankin
109 Regents Park Road
London NW1 8UR
0171 722 0997

Laura Ashley
0990 622116

MacCulloch & Wallis
25-6 Dering Street
London W1R 0BH
0171 629 0311

Malabar
31-3 The South Bank
 Business Centre
Ponton Road
London SW8 5BL
0171 501 4200

The Natural Fabric Company
Wessex Place
127 High Street
Hungerford
Berkshire RG17 0DL
01488 684002

Novatec
Unit 25
Leigh Road
Haine Industrial
 Estate
Ramsgate
Kent CT12 5EU
01843 850 666

Osborne & Little
304 Kings Road
London SW3 5UH
0171 352 1456

Romo
Lowmoor Road
Kirkby in Ashfield
Nottingham NG17 7DE
01623 756699

Rufflette
Sharston Road
Manchester M22 4TH
0161 998 1811

CRAFTS & ART MATERIALS

The Decorative Arts Company
5a Royal Crescent
London W11 4SL
0171 371 4303

Dylon
Dylon Consumer Advice
Worsley Bridge Road
Lower Sydenham
London SE26 5HD
0181 663 4296

The English Stamp Co.
 (rubber stamps)
Worth Matravers
Dorset BH19 3JP
01929 439117

Homecraft Direct
PO Box 38
Leicester LE1 9BU
0116 251 3139

Nu-Line (coir rope)
315 Westbourne Park Road
London W11 1EF
0171 727 7748

Paint Creative
17 Holywell Hill
St Albans
Hertfordshire AL1 1EZ
01727 836338

Susan Robertson Relief Stencilling
The Walled Garden
Dolforgan Hall
Kerry
New Town
Powys SY16 4DN
01686 670651

The Stencil Library
Stocksfield Hall
Stocksfield
Northumberland
NE43 7TN
01661 844844

MOULDINGS & ORNAMENTATIONS

Artefact
36 Windmill Street
London W1P 1HF
0171 580 4878

British Museum Catalogue
46 Bloomsbury Street
London WC1B 3QQ
0171 323 1234

Jali
Church Lane
Barham
Kent CT4 6QS
01227 831710

Lewis & Lewis
Units 7 & 8
Riverway Industrial Estate
Newport
Isle of Wight PO30 5UX
01983 524573

Richard Burbidge
Whittington Road
Oswestry
Shropshire SY11 1H3
01691 655131

Scumble Goosie
Lewiston Mill
Toadsmoor Road
Stroud
Gloucestershire GL5 2TB
01453 731305

Winther Browne
Mobel Road
London N18 3DX
0181 803 3434

GENERAL

After Noah
261 Kings Road
London SW3 5EL
0171 351 2610

Argos
0870 600 3030

Bhs
0171 262 3288

Cath Kidston
8 Clarendon Cross
London W11 4AP
0171 221 4000

Designers Guild
267-77 Kings Road
London SW3 5EN
0171 243 7300

Divertimenti (kitchenware)
139-41 Fulham Road
London SW3 6HH
0171 581 8065
0181 246 4300 (mail order)

Habitat
196 Tottenham Court Road
London W1P 9LD
0171 255 2545
0645 334433 (enquiries)

Heals
196 Tottenham Court Road
London W1P 9LD
0171 636 1666

The Holding Company
241-5 Kings Road
London SW3 5EL
0171 352 1600

41 Spring Gardens
Manchester M2 2BG
0161 834 3400

IKEA
255 North Circular Road
London NW10 0JQ
0181 208 5607

Inventory
26-40 Kensington High Street
London W8 4PF
0171 937 2626

Jerry's Home Store
163-7 Fulham Road
London SW3 6SN
0171 225 2246
0171 581 0909

Joanna Wood
48a Pimlico Road
London SW1 8LP
0171 730 5064

John Lewis
0171 629 7711

Lakeland
Alexandra Buildings
Windermere
Cumbria LA23 1BQ
01539 488100

Liberty
210-20 Regent Street
London W1R 6AH
0171 734 1234

Marks & Spencer
0171 935 4422

Muji
187 Oxford Street

London W1R 1AJ
0171 323 2208
0171 437 7503 (enquiries)

Neal Street East
5-7 Neal Street
London WC2H 9PU
0171 240 0135

Next
0116 284 9424
0345 100500 (mail order)

Paperchase
213 Tottenham Court Road
London W1P 9AF
0171 580 8496

The Pier
200 Tottenham Court
Road
London W1P 0AD
0171 814 5004

Selfridges
400 Oxford Street
London W1A 1AB
0171 629 1234

Shaker
322 Kings Road
London SW3 5U8
0171 352 3918

UNITED STATES

Crown City Hardware
1047 N. Allen Avenue
Pasadena
CA 91104
818 794 1188

Decorator's Supply
3610-12 S. Morgan Street
Chicago
IL 60609
773 847 6300

Home Trends Catalog
1450 Lyell Avenue
Rochester
NY 14606
716 254 6520

IKEA
Plymouth Commons
Plymouth Meeting
PA 19462
610 834 0150

Pottery Barn
PO Box 7044
San Francisco
CA 94120
800 922 5507

AUSTRALIA

BBC Hardware (branches
throughout NSW)
Cnr Cambridge and
Chester Streets
Epping
NSW 2121
02 9876 0888

Home Hardware (branches
throughout NSW)
15 Huntingwood Drive
Huntingwood
NSW 2148
02 9839 0777

Mitre 10 (branches
throughout VIC)
12 Dansu Court Hallam
Princess Highway
VIC 3803
03 9796 4999

True Value Hardware
(branches throughout SA
and QLD)
1367 Main North Road
Para West Hills
SA 5096
08 8281 2244

16 Cambridge Street
Rocklea
QLD 4106
08 3892 0892

Makit Hardware (branches
throughout WA)
87 President Street
Welshpool
WA 3966
08 9351 8001

NEW ZEALAND

Levene & Co Ltd
Harris Road
East Tamaki
09 274 4211

Mitre 10
169 Wairu Road
Glenfield
09 443 9900

Placemakers
Support Office
150 Marua Road
Panmure
09 535 5100

Addresses correct at time of
going to press.

INDEX

A

accessories, kitchen 44
alphabet
    letters on cushions
        124–5
    stencils 132–5

B

bag, drawstring
    126
banner-style
    pelmets 98–9
bar-fronted kitchen
    doors 51
bathrooms 14–15, 36–7,
    88
    classical opulence
        22–3
    Mediterranean style
        70–1
    seaside style 26–9
    tropical 68–9,
        114–15
batik 96–7
    bathroom curtains 22
beading 87
beads, added to throws
    126, 127
bedrooms
    stamped designs in
        10–13
    study-bedroom 18–21
below-stair storage 63
blinds 110–11
    bathroom 14, 114–15
    complementing muslin
        curtains 102
    and damp 114
    double-sided 104–5
    Roman 112–13

boxes, for
    storage 62–3
burlap see hessian
buttoned cushions 120

C

cabinets
    bathroom 80
    filing 57
    cake cutters, use in
        office 60
calligraphy
    decorative use in
        bathroom 22–3
    see also alphabet;
        letters
Caribbean effect,
    bathrooms 68–9,
        114–15
casters and mobility
    57, 63
ceramic paints on
    tiles 72, 73
chain, decorative 83
check pattern
    cupboard doors 53
    wallpaper 34–5
checked wallpaper see
    patchwork 34–5
chequerboard pattern
    floors 21
    walls 36–7
chicken-wire fronted doors
    see net-covered doors
classical details 84–5
clothes pegs, as curtain
    hooks 94–5
colour
    bathroom 14–15
    kitchen 44–5

colourwash bathroom
    15, 26–8
    panelling 28
    stripes in hall 16–17
computer equipment, and
    offices 59–60
containers, inexpensive 64
cool and frosted doors, in
    kitchens 49
corbels, plastic 80–1
country kitchens, storage
    in 64–5
cupboards
    decorative doors 46–53
    sliding doors 63
curtain, to disguise bath
    114–15
curtain clips 97
curtain poles
    unusual 94–5
    use in office storage 60
curtains
    for kitchen cupboards
        54–5
    on kitchen doors
        50, 54–5
Curtains & Blinds 91–115
cushions
    customized 120–1
    monogrammed 124–5
customized cushions
    120–1
customized shelves 74–7

D

damp and blinds 114
Decoration & Display
    67–89
decorative mouldings 30,
    82–9

Decorator's Essentials 129–39

découpage, wallpaper 32–3

display of utensils 64

distressing of shiplap
    boards 41

doorknobs, for curtain
    hanging 98–9

doors
    kitchen 46–7
    sliding, on cupboards 63

drapes *see* curtains

drawstring bag 126

dyeing
    batik method 97
    cushion covers 121
    muslin 103
    throws 123

E

edgings
    to blinds 117
    to shelves 74–5

entrances (hallways) 16–17

F

fabrics, to cover screens 118
    see also curtains

filing cabinets 57

finials, to curtain poles 94–5

finishing touches to
    decorating schemes 126–7

fleur-de-lys, moulded 89

floors
    chequerboard, painting
        21
    wooden hallways 16–17

folding screens *see* screens

frames, picture,
    inexpensive 89

frieze, découpage 32–3

furniture
    patchwork used on 34
    seaside style bathroom
        26–7

G

glass shelving 75

gold paint
    lettering 22–3
    on tiles 72

gothic arch, shape 84–5

grouting, coloured, for tiles 88

H

hairdryer, to dry paint 73

hall area, for storage 62–3

hallways 16–17

hearts, in kitchen doors 48

herbs and spices 54–5

hessian (burlap)
    blinds 104–5
    to cover screens 118

hinges, to kitchen
    doors 46

hooks, grid, use in office 59

I

image-making kit, for
    cushions 121

K

kitchens
    accessories 44
    country, storage in 64–5
    made over 44–55
    storage 44–5
    utensils 64

L

lace edging to blinds
    112

lampshades, decorative
    fabric 126–7

lettering 132–5
    on cushions 124–5
    see also calligraphy

light, effect on
    decoration 14

M

magnets, use in offices 59

maritime theme *see* seaside
    effects

masking tape and
    calligraphy 22
    use in colourwash
        striping 17
    use in floor painting
        21

matching 96

matting, herringbone,
    in bedroom 12

MDF (particleboard)
    bathroom 23, 68
    care needed in use
        39
    kitchen 44, 46
    offices 56
    for shelves 74, 75,
        76

Mediterranean-style
    bathroom 70–1

mesh, for kitchen
    doors 51

metal accessories, office
    furniture 58–60

metal loops, for curtain
    tiebacks 92

metallic paint 82, 87

mirrors
    rope-framed 70–1
    wavy-edged 68

modular storage 63

motifs for stencils 136–7

mouldings, prefabricated
    82–3, 84–5, 86–7

muslin 92–3, 102–3, 112
    dyeing 103

N

nautical effects *see* seaside
    effects

net-covered doors,
    kitchen 49, 54–5

noticeboard, office 57

O

offices, at home 56–61

P

paint
    ceramic 72, 73
    floorboard painting 21
    gold 22–3, 72
    metallic 82, 87

painting
    chequerboard floors 21
    large checks in
        bathroom 37
    skirting boards and
        window frames 12
    staircases 24–5

panelling 38–41
    colourwashing 28
    tongue-and-groove,
        bathroom 23, 26–7
    types 39

pans, storage 44–5

particleboard *see* MDF

pastel shades, in paint
    20

patchwork wallpaper
    34–5

peg rails 108–9

pelmets
    banner-style 98–9
    bathroom 26–7
    decorative 78, 84–5
    gathered 112
    matching blinds 106–7
    shaped, practical 107
    soft 100–1

Perspex (Plexiglass), in
    kitchen doors 49, 55

photograph cushions 121

picture rails 83

pictures in decorative
    schemes 89

pine, knotted, for hallway
    floors 16–17

pipe, metal, use as open
    wardrobe 63

plaster blocks,
    decorative 86

plastic mouldings 86–7

plate racks 75

playing card suit hooks 36,
    110–11

Plexiglass *see* Perspex

plotting path in painting
    plan 21

plumb line
    making one 37
    use 20

poles
    curtain 94–5, 100
    for kitchen storage 64
    for office storage 60
    and pipes 108

pots and pans,
    storage 44–5

practical tips 130–1

R

raffia tiebacks 92

rails and hooks, kitchen 44

refrigerators, disguised
    64

ribbons, as curtain ties 94

rope
    bathroom blind 114–15
    framing mirror 70–1

rubber stamps in
    bathroom 14–15
    decoration 10–13
    study bedroom 19
    technique 13

S

screens
    découpage on 32
    folding 118–19

sea shells *see* shells

seaside effects 26–9, 80,
    82, 89

Shaker style
    doors 46, 48
    and kitchens 46, 48, 54–5
    peg rails 108–9

shelf trim 39

shells 82, 84
    in decoration 70–1

shelves
    customizing 74–7
    office 57, 61

shiplap panelling
    39, 41

shower curtain rail 26–7

shower curtains 26

skirting boards,
    painting on staircases 24–5
Soft Furnishings 117–27
Space & Storage 43–65
special effects, and
    windows 80–1
spices and herbs, storage
    54–5
spiral designs 122–3
staircases
    below, storage 63
    painting steps 24–5
stamping, technique 10
    see rubber stamps
starfish motifs 68–9, 70–1
stars
    in batik decoration
        96–7
    in kitchen doors 50
stationery, office storage 60
stencilling
    behind shelves 76
    letters on cushions 124–5
    tiles 72–3
    wall 20
stencils
    alphabet 132–5
    bathroom 14, 26–7
    bathroom tiles 29
    bedroom 10
    use in calligraphy 22
    making 124
    motifs 136–7
    study-bedroom 18–19
    technique 20
    variety 19
    wooden staircases 24–5
steps *see* staircases
stick-on details 82–3
stockists 138–9
storage facilities, study-
    bedroom 18–19

stripes, colourwash in hall
    16–17
study-bedroom 18–19
style, achieved inexpensively
    88–9

T

table cloths, used as curtains
    94–5
tassels, in window decoration
    78
textures in bedroom 12
throws 122–3
    beaded 126, 127
    in bedroom 12
tiebacks for curtains
    92
tiles
    bathroom 14, 15
    clever use 88
    decorated 72–3
    in diamond shape
        22–3, 88
    effect using paint
        21
    stencilled bathroom
        26–7, 29
tiling of cupboard
    doors 53
timber *see* wood
tonal contrasts in
    stencilling 20
tongue-and-groove
    panelling 23, 26–7,
        28, 39
trellis
    in bathroom 36
    in kitchen 64
trompe l'oeil, cupboard
    fronts 52

tropical effects in bathroom
    68–9, 114–15

V

varnish, acrylic, for floors 21, 25
Velcro 107, 111, 112, 114

W

wall hooks, use in
    offices 56
wallpaper
    bathroom 14–15
    bedroom 10, 12
    découpage 32–3
    patchwork 34–5
    zigzag edge 30–1
Walls & Floors 9–41
    stencilling 20
wavy-edged mirror 68
windows, decorative
    treatment 78–9
wire cupboard doors
    see net-covered doors
wire baskets and
    cooling racks, office use
        58–9
wood
    floors in hallways 16–17
    planed timber in
        bathroom 23
words, for bathroom
    calligraphy 22
worktops 64

Z

zigzag edges, wallpaper
    30–1
    technique 31

PICTURE CREDITS

2 Rowland Roques-O'Neil; 5 Lucinda Symons;
8–37 Lucinda Symons; 38–40 Rowland Roques-O'Neil;
41 Lucinda Symons; 42–3 Steve Dalton; 43 inset
Lucinda Symons; 44–5 Rowland Roques-O'Neil;
46–53 Steve Dalton; 54–5 Rowland Roques-O'Neil;
56–63 Lucinda Symons; 64–5 Rowland Roques-O'Neil;
66–7 Lucinda Symons; 67 inset Spike Powell;
68–71 Spike Powell; 72–3 Rowland Roques-O'Neil;
74 Rowland Roques-O'Neil; 75 Lucinda Symons;
76–7 Rowland Roques-O'Neil; 78 Lucinda Symons;
79–81 Rowland Roques-O'Neil; 82 left Lucinda
Symons; 82 right Rowland Roques-O'Neil;
83–4 Lucinda Symons; 85 top Lucinda Symons;
85 bottom Rowland Roques-O'Neil; 86 Rowland
Roques-O'Neil; 86–7 top Lucinda Symons;
86–7 bottom Rowland Roques-O'Neil; 87 Lucinda
Symons; 88–9 Lucinda Symons; 90–1 Spike Powell;
91 inset Lucinda Symons; 92–5 Graham Seager;
96–7 Lucinda Symons; 98–101 Rowland Roques-O'Neil;
102–3 Spike Powell; 104–5 Lucinda Symons;
106–7 Rowland Roques-O'Neil; 108–9 Graham Seager;
110–11 Lucinda Symons; 112 top Graham Seager;
112 bottom Lucinda Symons; 113 Lucinda Symons;
114–15 Spike Powell; 116–17 Derek Lomas;
117 inset Lucinda Symons; 118–19 Lucinda Symons;
120–1 Rowland Roques-O'Neil; 122–3 Spike Powell;
124–5 Derek Lomas; 126–7 Lucinda Symons;
128–9 Lucinda Symons; 129 inset Rowland
Roques-O'Neil; 130–1 Lucinda Symons

Individual projects created and styled by Lucy Allnutt,
Denise Brock, Lisa Brown, Alison Davidson, Amanda
Morrison, Nicky Phillips, Gina Satch.

Front jacket photographs by Steve Dalton, Spike Powell,
Rowland Roques-O'Neil, Graham Seager, Lucinda
Symons.

Back jacket photographs by Spike Powell, Rowland
Roques-O'Neil, Lucinda Symons.

All photographs are copyright *House Beautiful*
magazine.

Stencil artworks on pages 136–7 by Pat McNeill.